ALFRED HITCHCOCK'S PSYCHO

Edited by Richard J. Anobile

A DARIEN HOUSE BOOK

 **FLARE BOOKS**/PUBLISHED BY AVON

A DARIEN HOUSE BOOK

AVON BOOKS
A division of
The Hearst Corporation
959 Eighth Avenue
New York, New York 10019

Published by arrangement with
Darien House, Inc.
37 Riverside Drive
New York City 10023

Library of Congress Catalog Card Number: 74-82131

ISBN 0-380-00085-7

First Flare Printing, September 1974.

FLARE TRADEMARK REG. U.S. PAT. OFF. AND
OTHER COUNTRIES. MARCA REGISTRADA,
HECHO EN U.S.A.

Printed in the United States of America

Introduction

PSYCHO is the first contemporary film in the Film Classics Library. Most film historians and buffs will argue against considering contemporary films as classics. But I view this attitude as unnecessarily shortsighted and fail to understand the reluctance of some individuals to recognize films produced today which will be classics thirty or forty years from their release.

Many of our most respected film historians have so buried themselves in the past that they are unable to appreciate and evaluate most contemporary filmmakers and their films. This is unfortunate. These historians are precisely the individuals to whom we should be able to look for perspective on current cinema. Instead, this burden unfairly falls upon the shoulders of daily film critics who cannot be expected to be as thorough in their perceptions. A daily critic's prime responsibility is to record current opinions in terms of current trends with an overall view towards performing a consumer service.

Over the last twenty years we have seen many new filmmakers produce what will no doubt be considered classics by future film historians. Some which come to mind are Penn's BONNIE AND CLYDE, Kubrick's DR. STRANGELOVE and 2001: A SPACE ODYSSEY, Truffaut's JULES AND JIM, Rydell's THE FOX, Coppola's THE CONVERSATION and Bertolucci's I CONFORMISTI. The list of contemporary classics is as mind-staggering as the collected accomplishments of Ford, Huston, Welles, and the host of other notables who are mentioned time and again. I intend The Film Classics Library to reflect this concept so as to be a useful tool for future filmmakers and a balanced record of developing cinema.

Alfred Hitchcock directed his first feature in 1922 (NUMBER THIRTEEN) and is still active today. He has transcended several generations of film audiences and his career has been marked by many hallmark films, one of which is PSYCHO.

A close look at PSYCHO reveals many of Hitchcock's secrets of film suspense. Storywise, the film is simple. But Hitchcock gives his audience a grand runaround and systematically catches the viewer off guard.

He first calls attention to the robbery of forty thousand dollars. The first reels of the film form an impression that all we are about to experience is another routine police drama. Will Janet Leigh get away with the money or has she unwittingly weaved a web for herself? Just when we think the film is running its presumed course, Hitchcock interferes and kills off the leading lady.

The shower scene is a classic. Over seventy camera setups of varying lengths come together to give cinema history one of its most harrowing sequences. Hitchcock was tampering with a personal, yet very common activity of everyday life. With forty-five seconds of grueling terror, he mesmerized viewers and imbued them with an immediate awareness of their own daily vulnerability during such an innocent habit. The stunned viewer tries to escape and overcome the horrible experience by running through earlier aspects of the film. Maybe there's a clue somewhere? But, alas, there is none.

The body is given a watery burial, along with the forty thousand dollars. The film is now off and running in a new direction. The only suspect is a little old lady known only to the viewer. At the same time we are confronted with a frantic Anthony Perkins who seems only to be protecting his eccentric mother; almost as American as apple pie!

Our allegiance switches from one character to another in a desperate search for something on which to grasp. Finally, to our relief, a private investigator enters the picture. Hitchcock obliges us with a series of dissolves picturing the busy detective questioning people all over town. Just as we finally settle down thinking we might get to the bottom of the case, the investigator gets himself killed in another gruesome and extremely cinematic murder.

Hitchcock is obviously having the time of his career. About all the viewer can count on is the haunting music by Bernard Herrmann. It's always there to heighten suspense and is our only clue that there is more to come. One marvelous use of the music, unfortunately lost in this book for obvious reasons, is its synchronization with the windshield wipers of Janet Leigh's car. As she becomes more and more nerve-racked, the music continually screeches until her relief at sighting Bates Motel. But here, too, Hitchcock lulls us into a false sense of security.

PSYCHO is full of red herrings and the viewer must ultimately pardon Hitchcock who by the end of the film ties all the loose ends into a nice neat bundle. This is uncinematically accomplished through the psychiatrist's monologue which must contain more dialogue than in all the preceding reels.

In 1960, Hitchcock was blazing new trails by presenting the most terrifying murder sequence ever shot on American celluloid. He set a trend that resulted in films such as Robert Aldrich's WHAT EVER HAPPENED TO BABY JANE? Today, that trend has been taken to the extreme and we find ourself assaulted with sometimes senseless screen violence by misguided directors who aim merely for sensationalism.

Hitchcock may have also been the first to introduce the brassiered leading lady to the American screen. Unfortunately, his boldness had to be later subdued and he was forced to censor the shower scene. Even today, the bottom of the screen is masked to prevent a glimpse of Janet Leigh's breasts. For this book, I had hoped to present an uncensored version if, in fact, one existed. But Universal Pictures, the current owner of the film, had only a masked version available for its use. William Hornbeck, head of Universal's editorial department, did his best to track down the original negative of the film but it seems to have been lost in the transfer from Paramount.

PSYCHO, as completed by Hitchcock, was at least a whole reel (about ten minutes) longer than the released version. Deleted are entire scenes and parts of others, all of which are indicated in the script continuity from which I worked. For instance, the sequence with the highway patrolman is shorter in the released version than in the continuity. Other shortened scenes include a longer telephone conversation between the sheriff and Norman and scenes between John Gavin and Vera Miles. Luckily, nothing deleted hurts the film and it was easy to see how the pace was quickened and the tension heightened by many of the deletions.

Here then is PSYCHO. Over 1400 frame blowups have been coupled with the original dialogue for a complete reconstruction of the film as released. Unlike other books in this series there are several stretches of pages without dialogue. In these instances I have selected more than the usual number of frames in order to facilitate a better flow for the reader. PSYCHO is probably Hitchcock's most visual film despite the simplicity of his direction. If he was to be judged by only this one work, he would still have to be considered the "master of suspense."

Richard J. Anobile
New York City
June, 1974

Acknowledgments

I would like to take this opportunity to thank those individuals whose cooperation have made this book possible.

Rights to produce this book were granted to us by Universal Pictures and Robert Bloch, author of the original novel. Steve Adler of Universal was especially helpful in sorting out legal tangles. Bill Hornbeck, who heads Universal's editorial department, deserves applause for getting things moving at his studio to facilitate getting print and negative materials to my editing studio in New York.

Alyne Model and George Norris of Riverside Film Associates transferred my marks to negative material and attended to the nitty-gritty of that highly technical job. All blowups were produced at Vita Print in New York City.

Harry Chester Associates was responsible for the design.

As always, I'd like to thank Stu Solow for seeing to it that typographical errors were deleted. And finally, Vivien Rowan at Darien House who goes slightly insane trying to keep my mayhem to a minimum.

Richard J. Anobile

Note to reader:

In keeping as true to the film as possible I have left in lap dissolves and fades where I felt they were necessary. The effect of a lap dissolve to the reader will be the appearance of two seemingly superimposed photos. The purpose here – as it was the director's, is to bridge the time and place gap between two scenes.

You will also notice a fuzziness in some frames. This is due to the fact that every photo is taken from blow-ups of the film itself. All possible means have been taken to insure clarity but inconsistencies in negative quality account for the variations of photo densities you will observe.

ALFRED HITCHCOCK'S

PSYCHO

DIRECTOR OF PHOTOGRAPHY   JOHN L. RUSSELL, A.S.C.

ART DIRECTION   JOSEPH HURLEY & ROBERT CLATWORTHY

SET DECORATOR   GEORGE MILO

UNIT MANAGER   LEW LEARY

TITLES DESIGNED BY   SAUL BASS

EDITED BY   GEORGE TOMASINI, A.C.E.

COSTUME SUPERVISOR   HELEN COLVIG

MAKE-UP SUPERVISION   JACK BARRON & ROBERT DAWN

HAIRSTYLIST   FLORENCE BUSH

SPECIAL EFFECTS   CLARENCE CHAMPAGNE

SOUND RECORDING BY   WALDON O. WATSON & WILLIAM RUSSELL

ASSISTANT DIRECTOR HILTON A. GREEN

PICTORIAL CONSULTANT SAUL BASS

MUSIC BY **BERNARD HERRMANN**

DIRECTED BY ALFRED HITCHCOCK

ALFRED HITCHCOCK

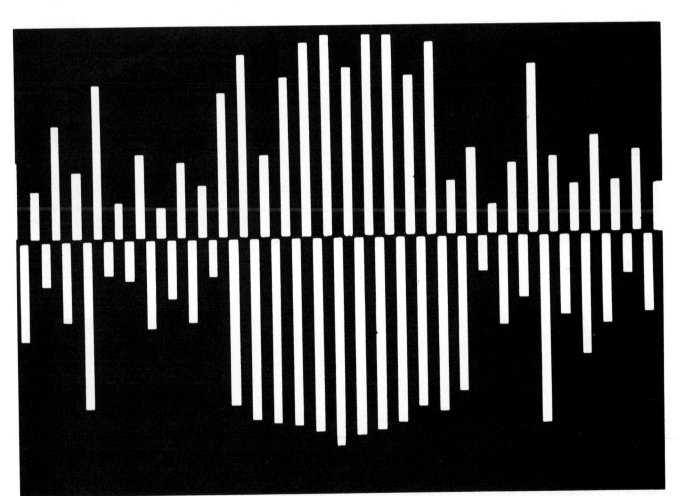

PHOENIX, ARIZONA

FRIDAY, DECEMBER THE ELEVENTH

TWO FORTY-THREE P.M.

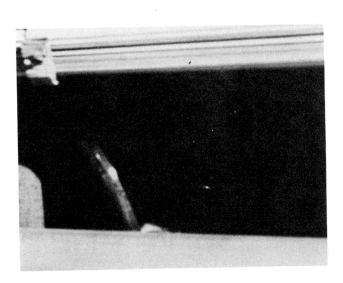 

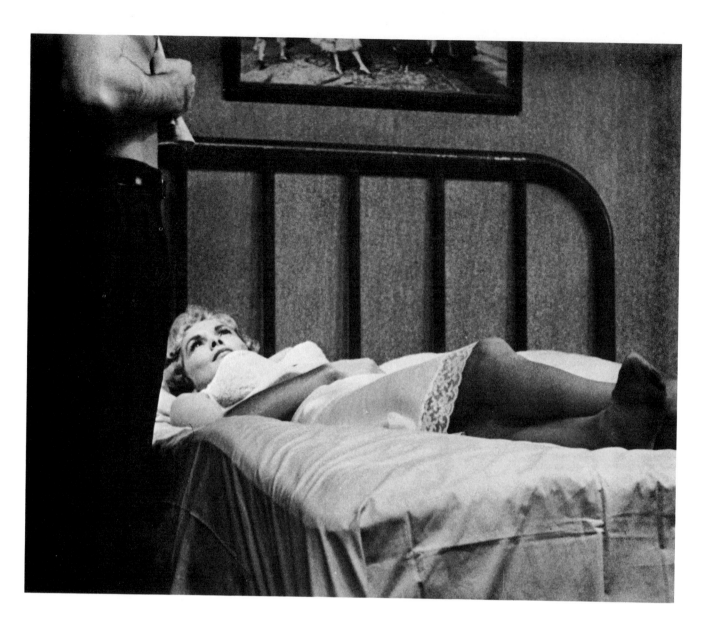

Sam: You never did eat your lunch, did you?

Marion: I better get back to the office. These extended lunch hours give my boss excess acid.

Sam: Why don't you call your boss and tell him you're taking the rest of the afternoon off? It's Friday, anyway—and hot.

Marion: What do I do with my free afternoon? Walk you to the airport?

Sam: We could laze around here a while longer.

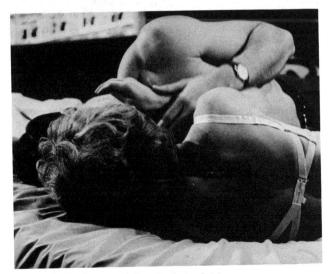

Marion: Checking out time is three P.M.

Marion: Hotels of this sort—are not interested in you when you come in, but when your time is up—Oh, Sam, I hate having to be with you in a place like this.

Sam: I've heard of married couples who deliberately spend an occasional night in a cheap hotel. They say it's very exciting—
Marion: Oh, when you're married you can do a lot of things deliberately.

Sam: You sure talk like a girl who's been married.
Marion: Sam—this is the last time.
Sam: Yeah? For what?

Marion: For this. For meeting you in secret—so we can be secretive. You come down here on those business trips and we steal lunch hours and—

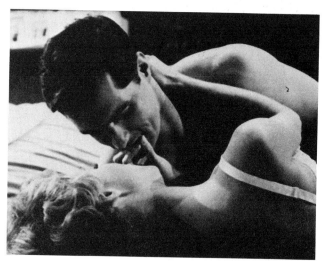

Marion: Oh, Sam, I wish you wouldn't even come.

Sam: All right. What do we do instead? Write each other lurid love letters?

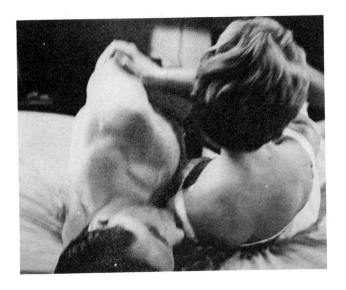 

Marion: I have to go, Sam.

Sam: I can come down next week.

Marion: No.
Sam: Not even just to see you? To have lunch—in public.
Marion: Oh, we can see each other.

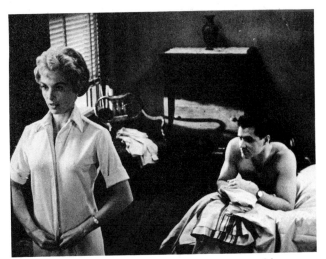

Marion: We can even have dinner—but respectably—

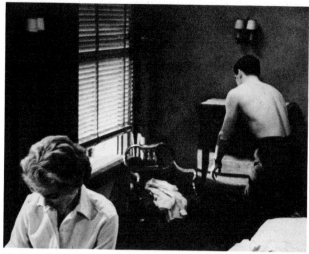

Marion: in my house with my mother's picture on the mantel and—

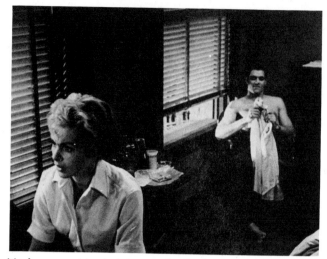

Marion: my sister helping me broil a big steak for three.

Sam: And after the steak, do we send Sister to the movies? Turn Mama's picture to the wall?

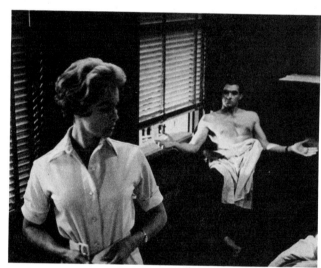

Marion: Sam!

Sam: All right!

Sam: Marion, whenever it's possible I want to see you. And under any circumstances.

Sam: Even respectability.

Marion: You make respectability sound—disrespectful.
Sam: Oh, no—I'm all for it! It requires patience, temperance—a lot of sweating-out. Otherwise, though, it's just hard work.

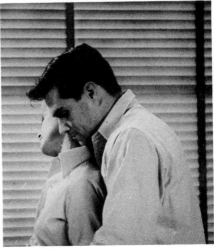

Sam: But if I can see you and touch you even as simply as this—I won't mind.

Sam: I'm tired of sweating for people who aren't there!

Sam: I sweat to pay off my father's debts and he's in his grave!

Sam: I sweat to pay my ex-wife alimony, and she's— living on the other side of the world somewhere!

Marion: I pay, too.

Marion: They also pay who meet in hotel rooms.

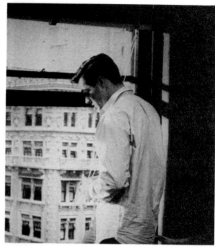

Sam: A couple of years and—the debts will be paid off and—if she ever remarries, the alimony stops and—

Marion: I haven't even been married once yet!

Sam: Yeah, but—when you do, you'll swing!

Marion: Sam, let's get married!

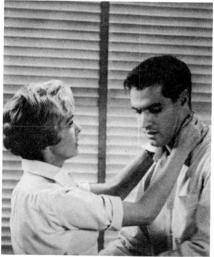

Sam: Yeah! And live with me in a storeroom behind a hardware store in Fairvale? We'll have lots of laughs!

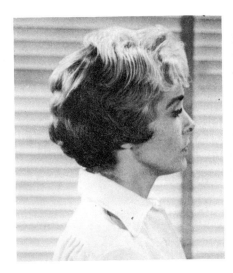

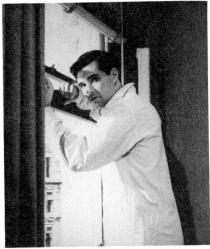

Sam: I tell you what. When I send my ex-wife alimony, you can lick the stamps!

Marion: I'll lick the stamps.

Sam: Marion, you want to cut this off— go out and find yourself somebody available?
Marion: I'm thinking of it.

Sam: How could you even think a thing like that?

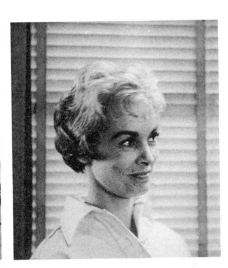

Marion: Don't miss your plane.

Sam: Hey, we can leave together, can't we?
Marion: Hm-mm. I'm late.

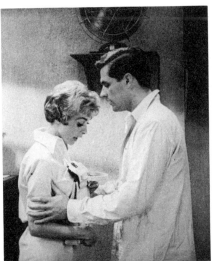

Marion: And uh—you have to put your shoes on.

21

Marion: Is Mr. Lowery back from lunch?

Caroline: He's lunching with the man who's buying the Harris Street property. You know—the oil lease man? That's why he's late. You got a headache?

Marion: Oh, it'll pass. Headaches are like resolutions— You forget them as soon as they stop hurting.

Caroline: Have you got some aspirin?
Marion: No.
Caroline: I've got something—not aspirin.

Caroline: My mother's doctor gave them to me the day of my wedding.

Caroline: Teddy was furious when he found out I'd taken tranquilizers!

Marion: There any calls?

Caroline: Teddy called me—my mother called to see if Teddy called.

Caroline: Oh, your sister called to say she's going to Tucson to do some buying

Caroline: and she'll be gone the whole weekend, and—

23

Cassidy: Wow! It's as hot as fresh milk!

Cassidy: Say, you girls oughtta get your boss to air-condition you up! He can afford it today.

Lowery: Oh, Marion, will you get the copies of that deed ready for Mr. Cassidy?

Cassidy: Yeah, tomorrow's the day! My sweet little girl.

Cassidy: Oh—oh, not—not you. My daughter. A baby!

Cassidy: And tomorrow she stands her sweet self up there and gets married away from me.

Cassidy: Ah—I want you to take a look at my baby.

Cassidy: Eighteen years old—

Cassidy: and she never had an unhappy day in any one of those years!

Lowery: Come on, Tom. My office is air-conditioned.

Cassidy: Do you know what I do about unhappiness? I buy it off. Are uh—are you unhappy?

Marion: Uh—not inordinately.

Cassidy: I'm buying this house for my baby's wedding present. Forty thousand dollars, cash!

Cassidy: Now that's—that's not buying happiness. That's just—buying off unhappiness.

Cassidy: I never carry more than I can afford to lose! Count 'em!

Caroline: I declare!

Cassidy: I don't! That's how I get to keep it!

Lowery: Tom, uh—cash transactions of this size! Most irregular!

Cassidy: Oh, so what? It's my private money! Now it's yours!

Lowery: Uh—suppose we put it in the safe and then—
Monday morning when you're feeling good—

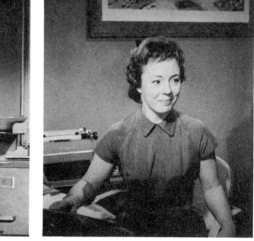

Cassidy: Oh, speaking of feeling good,
where's that bottle you said was in your
desk?

Cassidy: Oh-oh!

Cassidy: You know, uh—sometimes I can keep my mouth
shut.

Cassidy: Lowery, I am dying of thirstaroonie!

Lowery: I don't even want it in the office over the week-end. Put it in the safe deposit box in the bank and—

Lowery: we'll get him to give us a check on Monday instead.

Caroline: He was flirting with you.

Caroline: I guess he must have noticed my wedding ring.

Lowery: Come in.

Marion: The copies.

Marion: Uh—Mr. Lowery, if you don't mind, I'd like to go right on home after the bank. I have a slight headache.

30

Cassidy: You go right on home! Because me and your boss are goin' out and get ourselves a little drinkin' done! Right?

Lowery: Uh—of course. Do you feel ill?
Marion: Uh—just a headache.

Cassidy: Well, what you need is a week-end in Las Vegas—the playground of the world!

Marion: I'm going to spend this week-end in bed. Thank you.

Caroline: Aren't you going to take the pills? They'll knock that headache out.

Marion: Can't buy off unhappiness with pills! I guess I'll go put this money in the bank,—then go home and sleep it off.

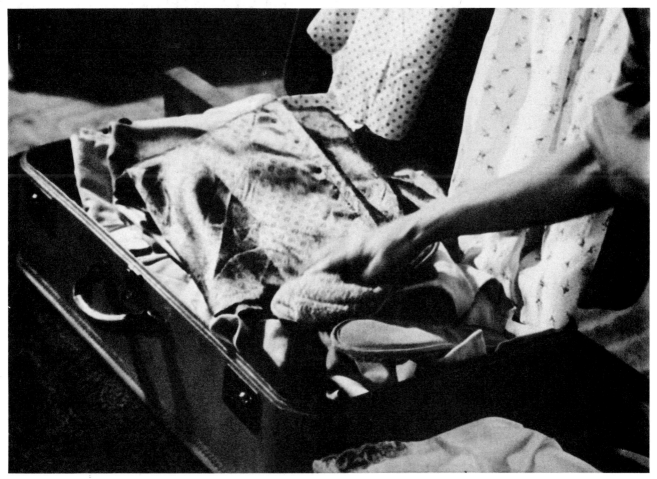

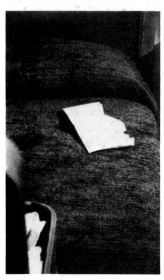

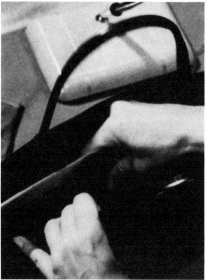

 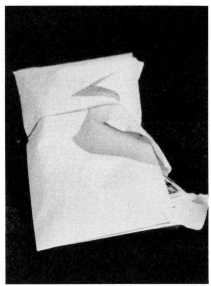 

 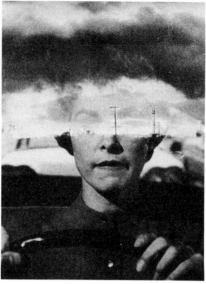 

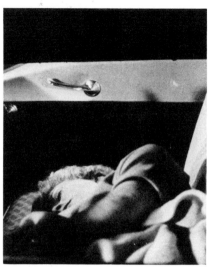

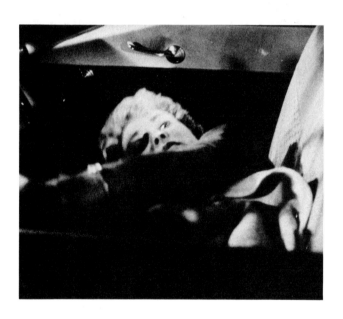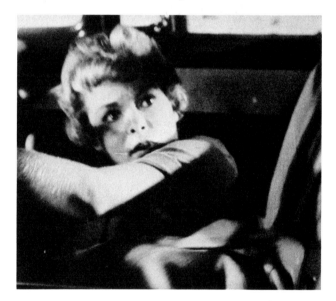

Patrolman: Uh—hold it there!

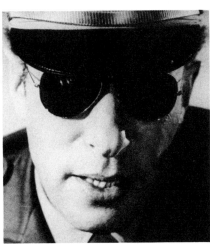

Patrolman: In quite a hurry.

Marion: Yes. Uh—I didn't intend to sleep so long. I almost had an accident last night, from sleepiness. So I decided to pull over.

Patrolman: You slept here all night?

Marion: Yes. As I said, I couldn't keep my eyes open.

Patrolman: There are plenty of motels in this area. You should've—I mean, just to be safe—

Marion: I didn't intend to sleep all night! I just pulled over. Have I broken any laws?

Patrolman: No, ma'am.
Marion: Then I'm free to go?

Patrolman: Is anything wrong?
Marion: Of course not. Am I acting as if there's something wrong?

Patrolman: Frankly, yes.
Marion: Please—I'd like to go.
Patrolman: Well, is there?

Marion: Is there what? I've told you there's nothing wrong,—except that I'm in a hurry and you're taking up my time.

Patrolman: Now, just a moment! Turn your motor off, please.

Patrolman: May I see your license?

Marion: Why?
Patrolman: Please.

Car Dealer: Be with you in a second!

Car Dealer: I'm in no mood for trouble.
Marion: What?
Car Dealer: There's an old saying, "First customer of the day is always the most trouble!"

Car Dealer: But like I say, I'm in no mood for it so I'm gonna treat you so fair and square that you won't have one human reason to give me—

Marion: Can I trade my car in and take another?
Car Dealer: Do anything you've a mind to. Bein' a woman, you will. That yours?

Marion: Yes, it's just that—there's nothing wrong with it. I just—
Car Dealer: Sick of the sight of it! Well, why don't you have a look around here and see if there's somethin' that strikes your eyes

Car Dealer: and meanwhile I'll have my mechanic give yours the once over. You want some coffee? I was just about—

Marion: No, thank you. I'm in a hurry. I just want to make a change, and—
Car Dealer: One thing people never oughtta be when they're buyin' used cars and that's in a hurry.

 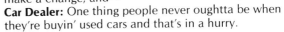

Car Dealer: But like I said, it's too nice a day to argue. I'll uh—shoot your car in the garage here.

Car Dealer: That's the one I'd've picked for you myself.

Marion: Uh—how much?

Car Dealer: Go ahead and spin it around the block.

Marion: It looks fine. How much will it be with my car?

Car Dealer: You mean you don't want the usual day and a half to think it over? Hah! You are in a hurry, aren't you? Somebody chasin' you?

Marion: Of course not. Please.

Car Dealer: Well,—it's the first time a customer has ever high-pressured the salesman! Uh—I'd figure roughly— your car plus seven hundred dollars.
Marion: Seven hundred.

Car Dealer: Ah,—you always got time to argue money, uh?

Marion: All right.

Car Dealer: I take it you can prove that car is yours—I mean, uh—out of state license and all. You got your pink slip and—

Marion: I believe I have the necessary papers. Is there a Ladies' Room?

Car Dealer: In the building.

Car Dealer: I think you'd better take it for a trial spin. Don't want any bad word of mouth about California Charlie.

Marion: I'd really rather not. Uh—can't we just settle this?
Car Dealer: I—might as well be perfectly honest with you, ma'am. It's not that I don't trust you, but uh—

Marion: But what? Is there anything so terribly wrong about—making a decision and wanting to hurry! Do you think I've stolen my car?

Car Dealer: No, ma'am. All right. Let's go inside.

53

Mechanic: Hey!

Marion: Oh, just put it in here, please. Thank you.

Car Dealer's Voice: *Heck, Officer, that was the first time I ever saw the customer high-pressure the salesman! Somebody chasin' her?*
Patrolman's Voice: *I better have a look at those papers, Charlie.*

Car Dealer: *She look like a wrong-one to you?*
Patrolman: *Acted like one.*
Car Dealer: *The only funny thing, she paid me seven hundred dollars in cash.*

Caroline's Voice: *Yes, Mr. Lowery?*
Lowery's Voice: *Caroline? Marion still isn't in?*
Caroline: *No, Mr. Lowery. But then, she's always a bit late on Monday mornings.*
Lowery: *Buzz me the minute she comes in.*

Lowery: *Then call her sister—if no one's answering at the house.*

Caroline: *I called her sister, Mr. Lowery, where she works,—the Music Makers Music Store, you know,—and she doesn't know where Marion is any more than we do.*

Lowery: *You'd better run out to the house. She may be, well—unable to answer the phone.*
Caroline: *Her sister's going to do that. She's as worried as we are.*

56

Lowery: *No, I haven't the faintest idea. As I said, I last saw your sister when she left this office on Friday. She said she didn't feel well and wanted to leave early; I said she could. That was the last I saw—Now wait a minute. I did see her sometime later, driving—Ah, I think you'd better come over here to my office—quick! Caroline, get Mr. Cassidy for me!*

Lowery: *After all, Cassidy, I told you—all that cash! I'm not taking the responsibility! Oh, for heaven's sake! A girl works for you for ten years, you trust her! All right. Yes. You better come over.*

Cassidy's Voice: *Well, I ain't about to kiss off forty thousand dollars! I'll get it back, and if any of it's missin' I'll replace it with her fine, soft flesh! I'll track her, never you doubt it!*

Lowery: *Oh, hold on, Cassidy! I-I still can't believe—It must be some kind of a mystery. I-I can't—*

Cassidy: *You checked with the bank, no? They never laid eyes on her, no? You still trustin'? Hot creepers! She sat there while I dumped it out! Hardly even looked at it! Plannin'! And—and even flirtin' with me!*

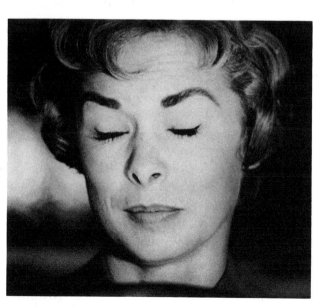 

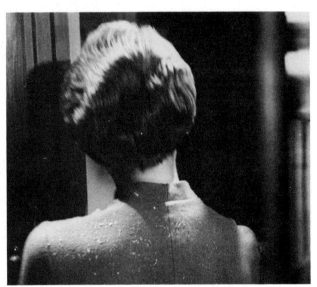

Norman: Dirty night.

Marion: Do you have a vacancy?
Norman: Oh, we have twelve vacancies.

Norman: Twelve cabins—twelve vacancies. They uh—
they moved away the highway.

Marion: Oh, I thought I'd gotten off the main road.

Norman: I knew you must have. Nobody ever stops here
anymore unless they've done that.

Norman: Well—there's no sense dwelling on our losses.

Norman: We just keep on lighting the lights and following the formalities.

Norman: Your home address. Oh, just the town will do.

Marion: Los Angeles.

Norman: Cabin One.

Norman: It's close in case you want anything. It's right next to the office.

Marion: I want sleep more than anything else. Except maybe, food.

Norman: Well, there's a big diner about ten miles up the road. Just outside of Fairvale.

Marion: Am I that close to Fairvale?
Norman: Fifteen miles. I'll get your bags.

Norman: Boy, it's stuffy in here.

Norman: Well, the uh—mattress is soft and—

Norman: there's hangers in the closet and stationery with 'Bates Motel' printed on it, in case you want to make your friends back home feel envious,

Norman:—and the uh—

Marion: The bathroom.

Norman: Yes. Well, uh—i-i-if you want anything just— just tap on the wall.

Norman: I'll—I'll be in the office.

Marion: Uh, thank you, Mr. Bates.

Norman: Norman Bates.

Norman: You're not really gonna go out again and drive up to the diner, are you?

Marion: No.

Norman: Well, then, would you do me a favor? Would you have dinner with me? I was just about to, myself. You know, nothing special.

Norman: Just sandwiches and milk. But I'd like it very much if you'd come up to the house.

Norman: Well, I—I don't set a fancy table but the kitchen's awful homey.

68

Marion: I'd like to.

Norman: All right. Uh—y-you get yourself settled, and— and take off your wet shoes,

Norman: and I'll be back as soon as it's ready,—with my—   **Norman:** with my trusty umbrella.

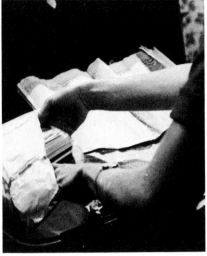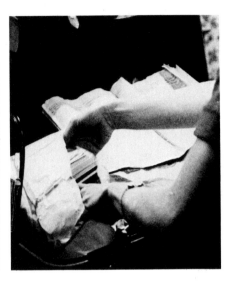
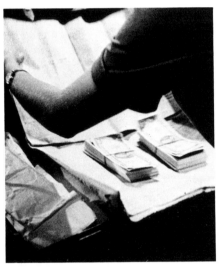

Woman: No! I tell you no! I won't have you bringing strange young girls in here for supper—

Woman: by candlelight, I suppose, in the cheap erotic fashion of young men with cheap, erotic minds!
Norman: Mother, please!

Woman: And then what, after supper? Music? Whispers?
Norman: Mother, she's just a stranger! She's hungry and it's raining out.

Woman: 'Mother, she's just a stranger!' As if men don't desire strangers! Ah! I refuse to speak of disgusting things, because they disgust me! Do you understand, boy?

Woman: Go on! Go tell her she'll not be appeasing her ugly appetite with my food, or my son! Or do I have to tell her 'cause you don't have the guts? Huh, boy? You have the guts, boy?
Norman: Shut up! Shut up!

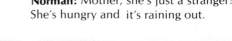

Marion: I've caused you some trouble.

Norman: No. Uh—uh, Mother—m-my Mother, uh—What is the phrase? 'She isn't quite herself today.'

Marion: You shouldn't have bothered. I really don't have that much of an appetite.

Norman: Oh, I'm sorry. Uh—I wish you could apologize for other people.

Marion: Don't worry about it. But as long as you've fixed the supper, we may as well eat it.

Norman: It uh—it—it might be uh—nicer—uh-uh—and warmer—in the office.

Marion: Well, it stopped raining.
Norman: Eating in an office is just—just too officious.
Uh—I-I-I—I have the parlor back here.

Marion: All right. Uh—

Norman: Sit down.

Marion: Oh—thank you. You're very kind.

Norman: It's all for you. I'm not hungry. Go ahead.

Norman: You—you eat like a bird.

Marion: And you'd know, of course.

Norman: No, not really. Anyway, I hear the expression 'eats like a bird'—it-it's really a fals—fals-fals—falsity. Because birds really eat a tremendous lot.

Norman: But—I—I don't really know anything about birds. My hobby is stuffing things. You know—taxidermy.

Norman: And I guess I'd—just rather stuff birds because—I hate the look of beasts when they're stuffed.

Norman: You know, foxes and chimps and—some—some people even stuff dogs and cats. But—Oh, I can't do that.

Norman: I—I think—I think only birds look well stuffed because—Well, because they're kinda—passive—to begin with.

Marion: It's a strange hobby. Curious.

Norman: Uncommon, too.

Marion: Oh, I imagine so.

Norman: And it's uh—it's not as expensive as you'd think. It's cheap, really. You know—needles and thread —sawdust. The chemicals are the only thing that uh—that cost anything.

Marion: A man should have a hobby.

Norman: Well, it's—it's-it's more than a hobby. A hobby's supposed to pass the time—not fill it.
Marion: Is your time so empty?

Norman: No. Uh—Well, I—I run the office, and uh— tend the cabins and grounds, and—and do little uh— errands for my mother,—the ones she allows I might be capable of doing.
Marion: Uh, do you go out with friends?

Norman: Well, uh—a boy's best friend is his mother.

Norman: You've never had an empty moment in your entire life, have you?
Marion: Only my share.
Norman: Where are you going?

Norman: I didn't mean to pry.
Marion: Hm. I'm looking for a private island.

Norman: What are you running away from?

Marion: Well, why do you ask that?

Norman: No. People never run away from anything. The rain didn't last long, did it?

Norman: You know what I think? I think that—we're all in our private traps— clamped in them.

Norman: And none of us can ever get out. We—we scratch and claw, but—only at the air—only at each other. And for all of it, we never budge an inch.

Marion: Sometimes we deliberately step into those traps.
Norman: I was born in mine. I don't mind it anymore.
Marion: Oh, but you should. You should mind it!

Norman: Oh, I do—but I say I don't.

Marion: You know—if anyone ever talked to me the way I heard—the way she spoke to you—

Norman: Sometimes—when she talks to me like that—I feel I'd like to go up there—and curse her—and-and-and leave her forever! Or at least defy her!

Norman: But I know I can't. She's ill.

Marion: She sounded strong.

Norman: No, I mean—ill. She—she had to raise me—all by herself, after my father died. I was only five and it—it must've been quite a strain for her.

Norman: I mean, she didn't have to go to work or anything like that. He left her a little money. Anyway, — a few years ago, Mother met this man.

Norman: And he—he talked her into building this motel. He could've talked her into anything.

Norman: And—when he died, too, it was—just too great a shock for her. And—and the way he died—

Norman: I guess it's nothing to talk about while you're eating. Anyway, it was just too great a loss for her. She had nothing left.

Marion: Except you.

Norman: Well, a son is a poor substitute for a lover.

Marion: Why don't you go away?

Norman: To a private island, like you?

Marion: No—not like me.

Norman: I couldn't do that. Who'd look after her? She'd be alone up there. The fire would go out.

Marion: Wouldn't it be better—if you put her—someplace?

Norman: You mean an institution? A madhouse?

Norman: It'd be cold and damp like a grave. If you love someone, you don't do that to them, even if you hate them. You understand that—I don't hate her. I hate what she's become. I hate the illness.

Norman: People always call a madhouse 'someplace' don't they? Put her in 'some place!'

Marion: I'm sorry. I didn't mean it to sound uncaring.

Norman: What do you know about caring?

Norman: Have you ever seen the inside of one of those places? The laughing and the tears—and the cruel eyes studying you?

Norman: My mother there? But she's harmless.

Norman: Why—she's as harmless as one of those stuffed birds.

Marion: I am sorry. Uh—I only felt—it seemed she's hurting you. I meant well.

Norman: People always mean well. They cluck their thick tongues and shake their heads and suggest—Oh, so very delicately—

Norman: Of course, I—I've suggested it myself. But I hate to even think about it. She needs me.

Norman: It-it-it's not as if she were a—a maniac—a raving thing—She just goes a little mad sometimes.

83

Norman: We all go a little mad sometimes. Haven't you?

Marion: Yes. And sometimes, just one time can be enough. And thank you.

Norman: Thank you, 'Norman.'

Marion: Norman.

Norman: Oh, y-you're not uh—You're not going back to your room already?

Marion: I'm very tired. And I'll have a long drive tomorrow. All the way back to Phoenix.

84

Norman: Really?

Marion: I stepped into a private trap back there—I'd like to go back and try to pull myself out of it,—

Marion: before it's too late for me, too.
Norman: Are you sure you wouldn't like to stay just a little while longer?

Norman: I mean—just for talk?

Marion: Oh, I'd like to, but—

Norman: All right. Well, uh—I'll see you in the morning. I'll bring you some breakfast. All right? What time?

Marion: Very early. Dawn.
Norman: All right, Miss uh—
Marion: Crane.

Norman: Crane. That's it.

Marion: Good night.

 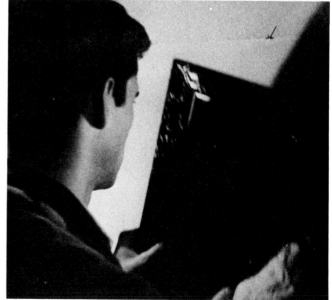

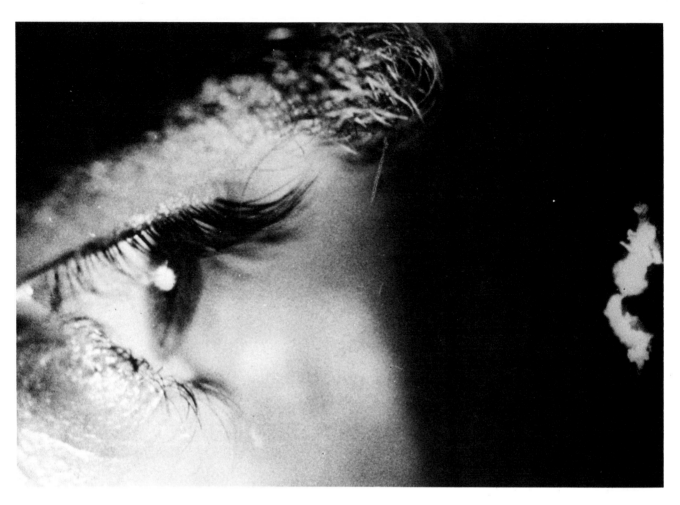

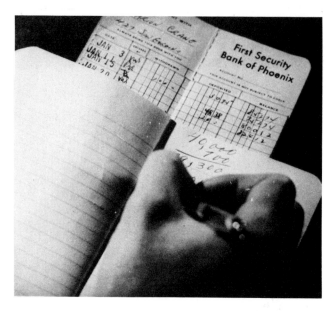

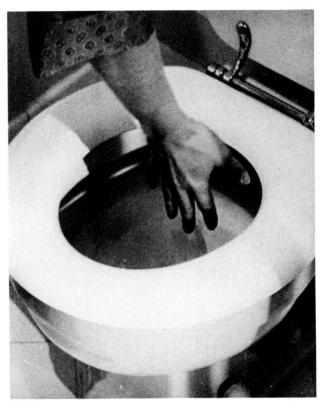

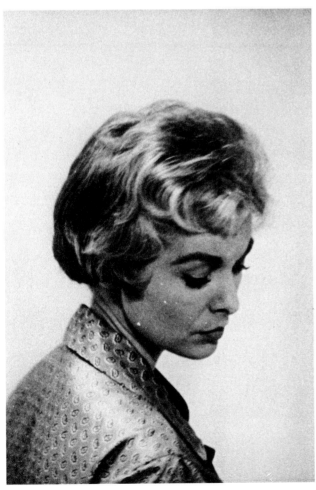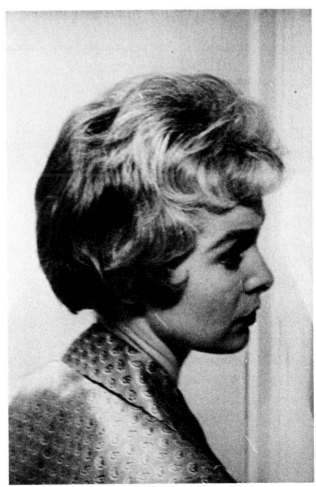

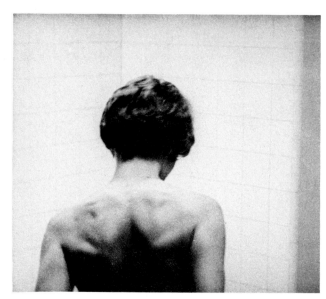

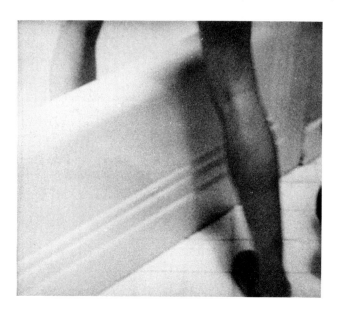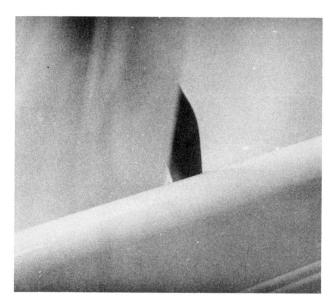

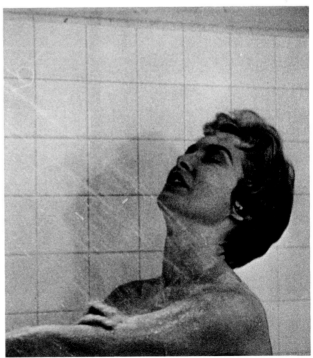

 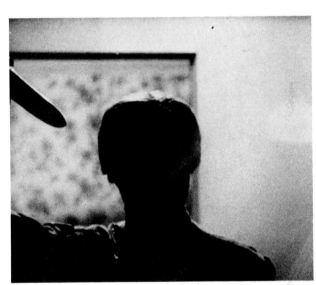

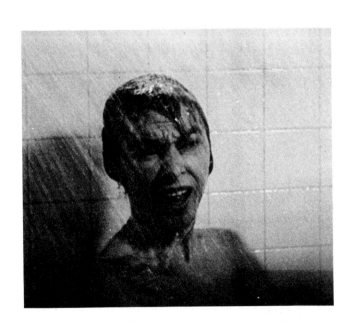 

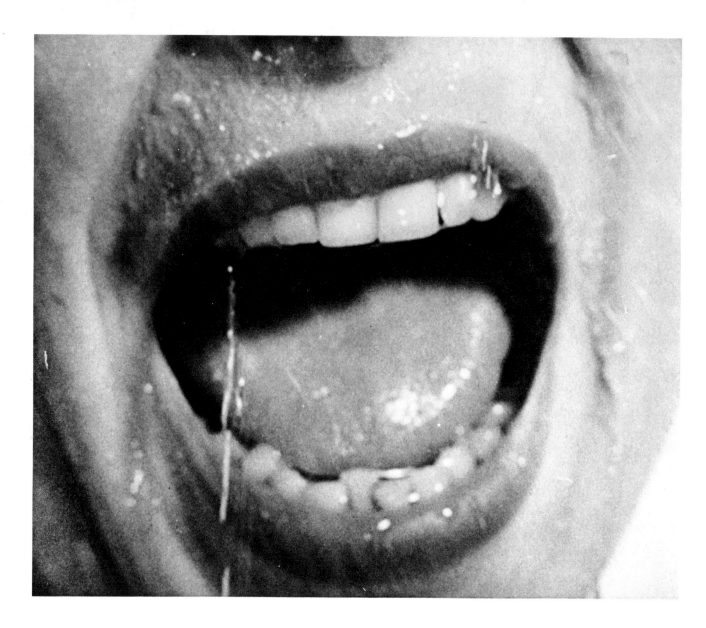

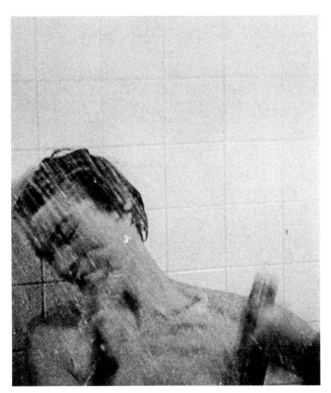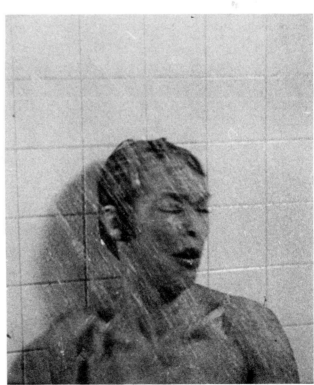

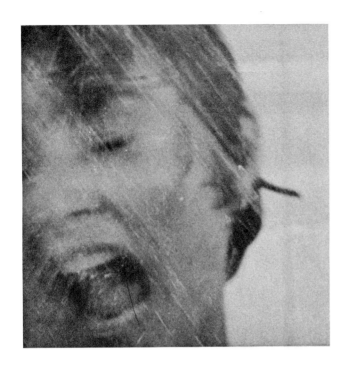

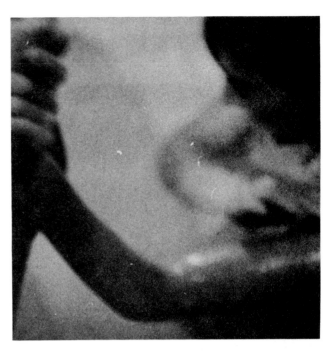

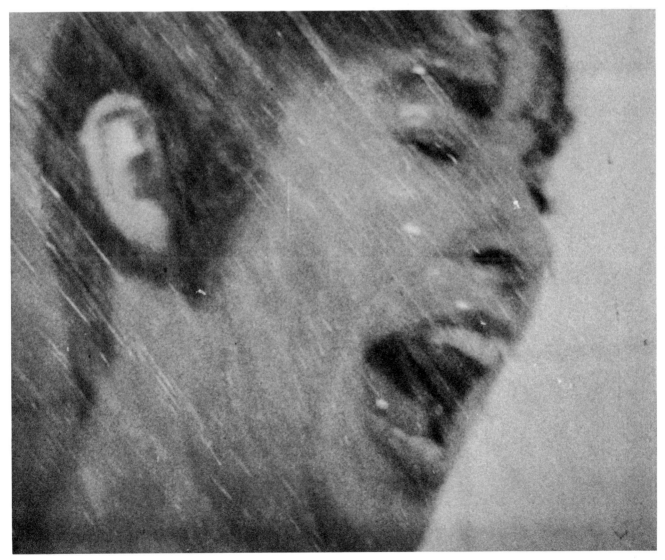

 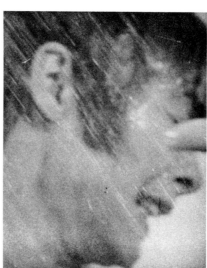 

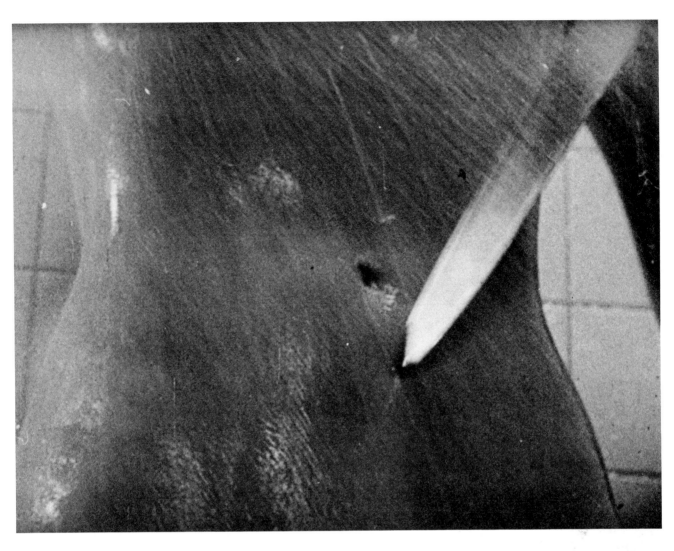

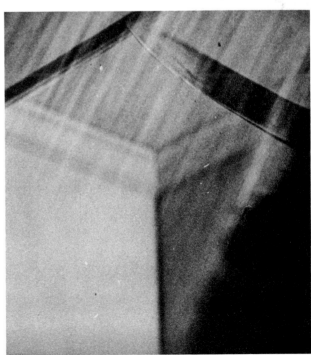

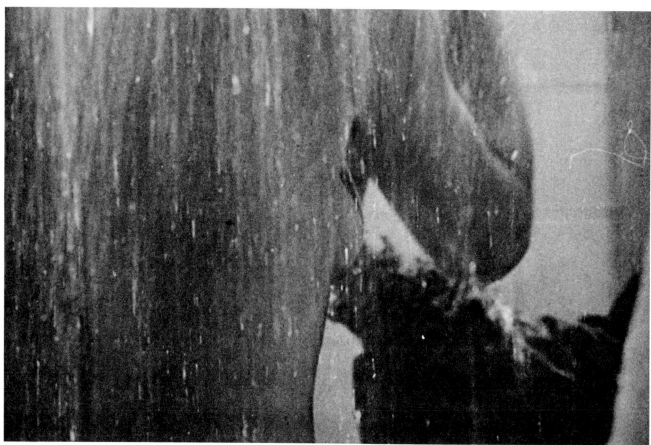

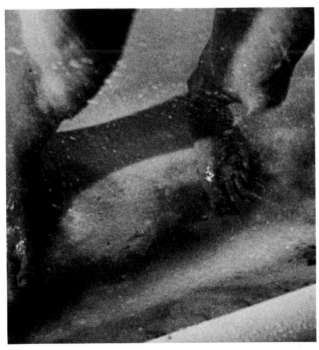

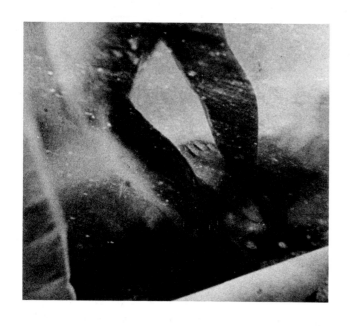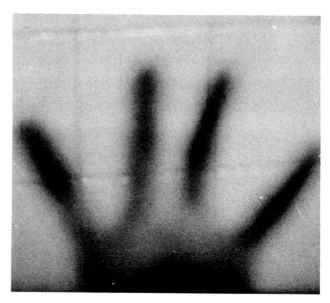

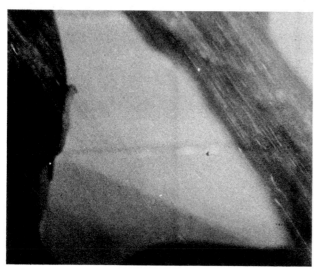

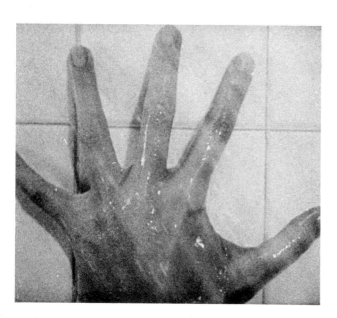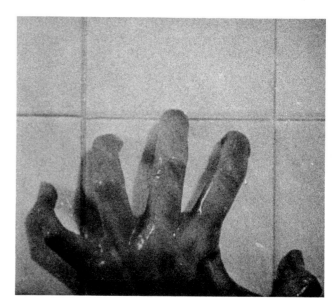

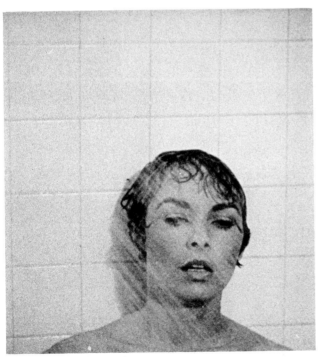

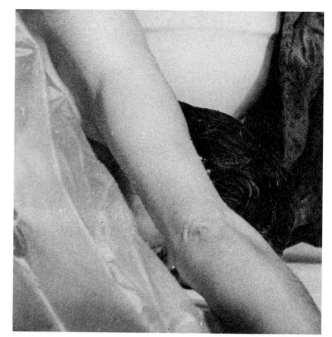

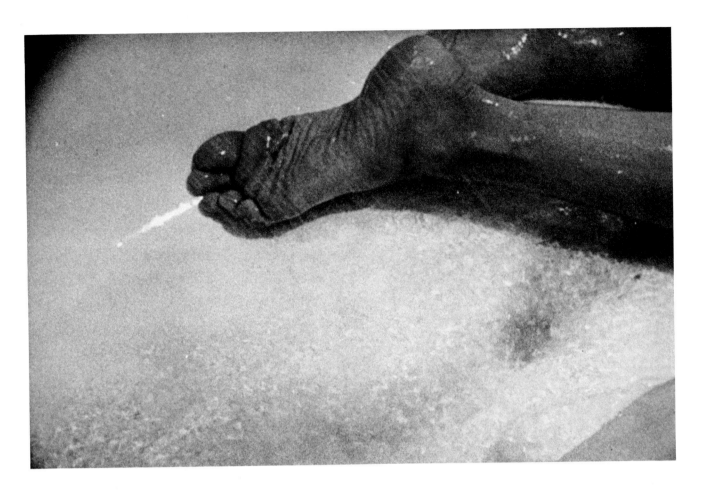

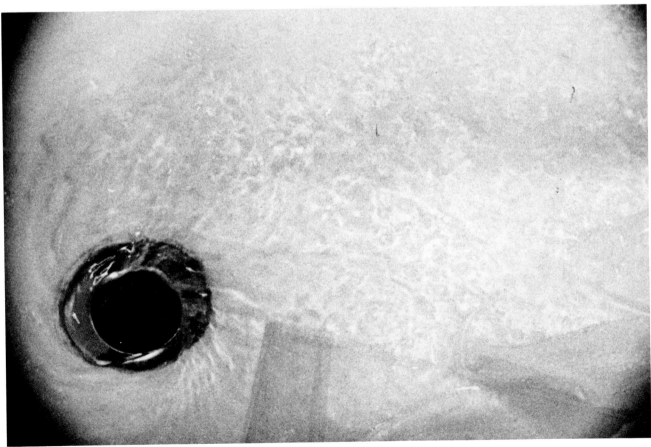

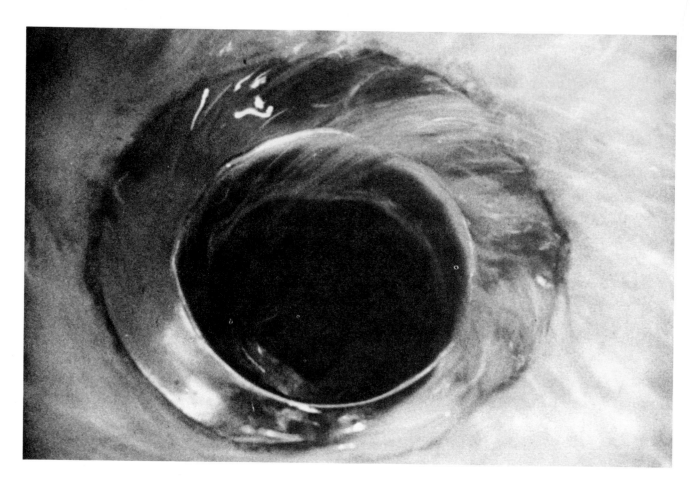

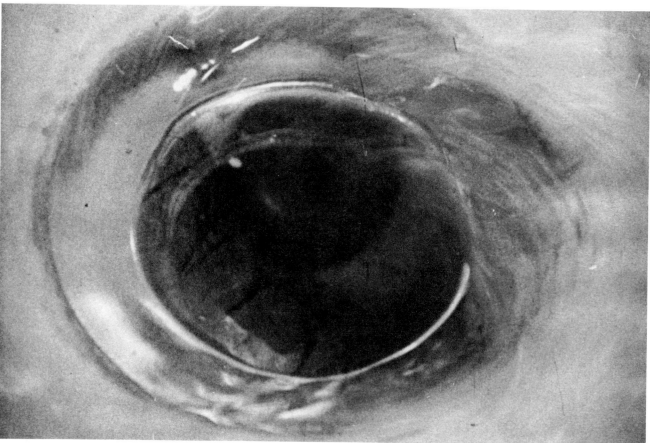

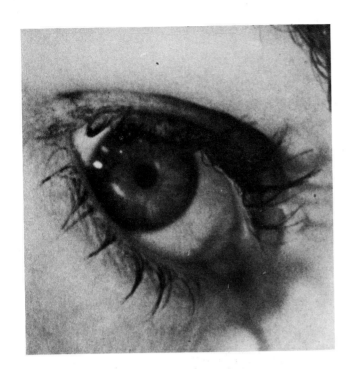

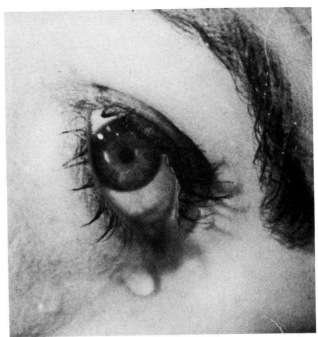

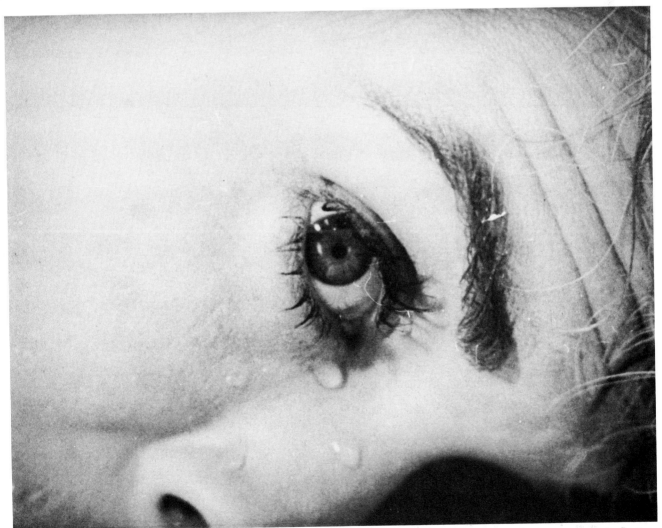

 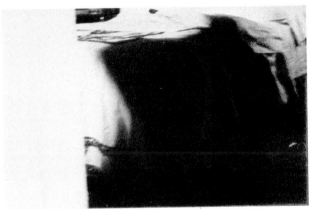

Norman: Mother! Oh God! Mother, mother! Blood, blood!

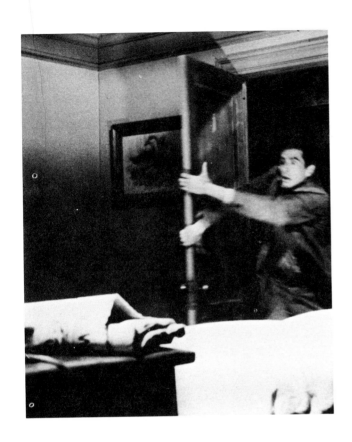

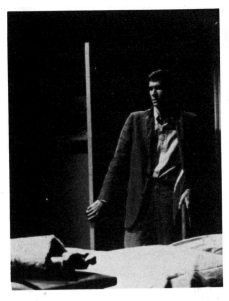

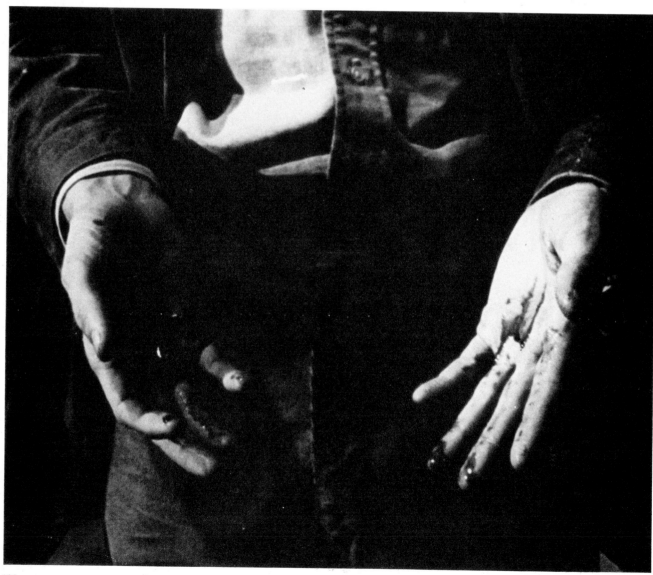

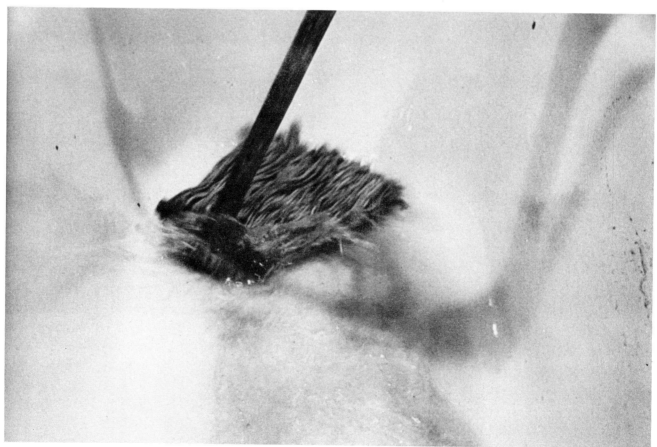

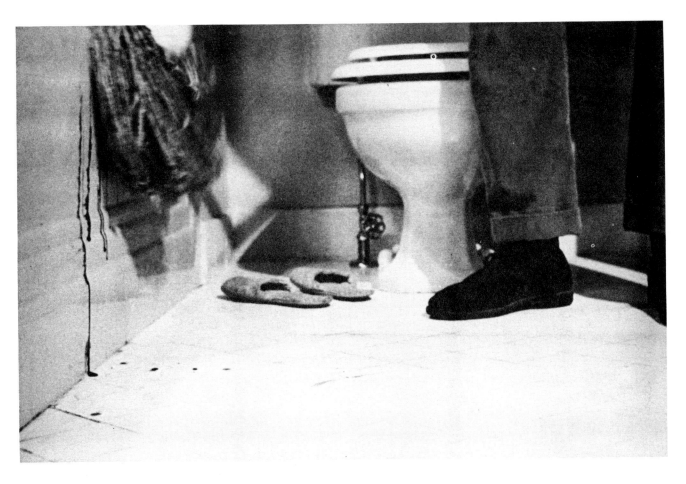

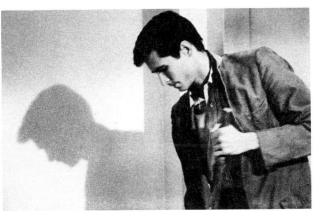

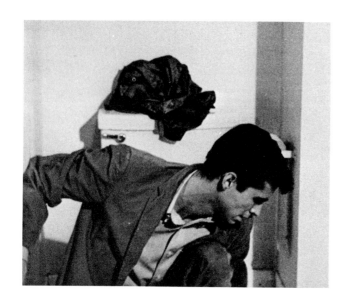

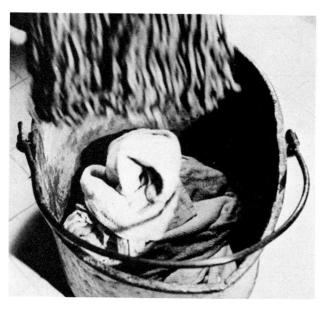

 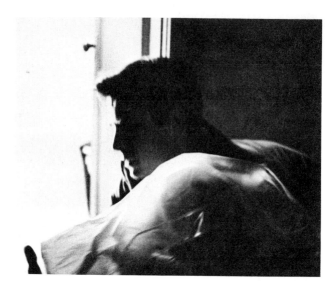

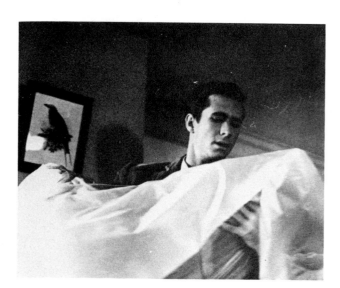 

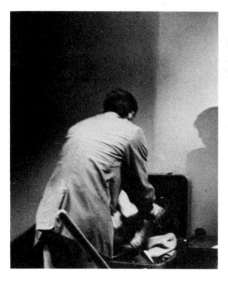  

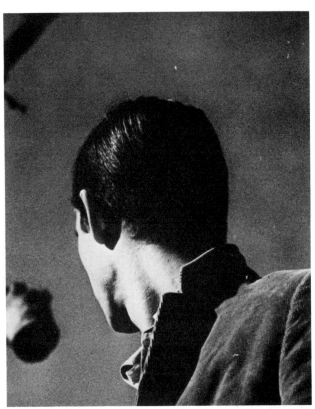

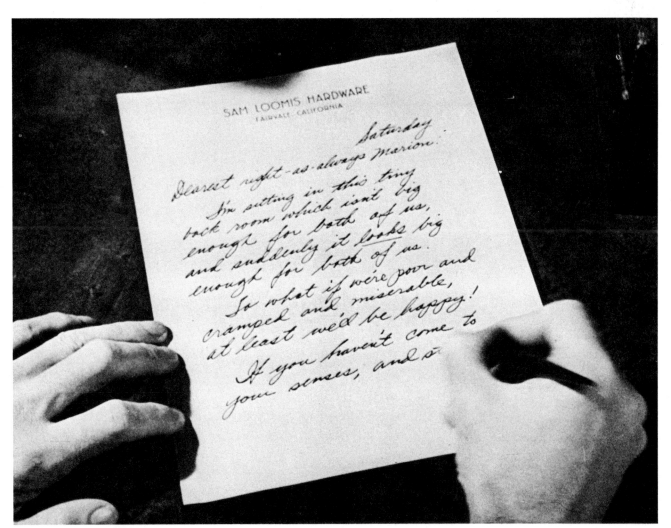

Woman: They tell you what its ingredients are,

Woman: and how it's guaranteed to exterminate every insect in the world,

Woman: but they do not tell you whether or not it's painless.

Woman: And—and I say, insect or man,

Woman: death should always be painless.

Lila: Sam?

140

Summerfield: Sam! Lady wants to see you!

Sam: Yes, miss?
Lila: I'm Marion's sister.
Sam: Oh, sure—Lila!

Lila: Is Marion here?
Sam: Why, of course, not! Something wrong?

Lila: She left home on Friday. I was in Tucson over the weekend and I haven't heard from her since,—not even a phone call.

Lila: Look, if you two are in this thing together, I don't care! It's none of my business.

Lila: But I want to talk to Marion and I want her to tell me it's none of my business! And then I'll go—

Sam: Bob! Run out and get yourself some lunch, will you?

Summerfield: Oh, that's okay, Sam. I brought it with me.

Sam: Run out and eat it!

Sam: Now—what thing could we be in together?
Lila: Sorry about the tears.

Sam: Well, is Marion in trouble? What is it?

Arbogast: Let's all talk about Marion, shall we?

Sam: Who are you, friend?

Arbogast: My name is Arbogast, friend. I'm a private investigator. Where is she, Miss Crane?

Lila: I don't know you.
Arbogast: Oh, well, I know you don't, because if you did I wouldn't be able to follow you.

Sam: What's your interest in this?
Arbogast: Well, uh—forty thousand dollars.
Sam: Forty thousand dollars?
Arbogast: That's right.

Sam: Well, one of you better tell me what's going on and tell me fast! I can take just so much of this and I—

Arbogast: Now take it easy, friend. Take it easy. You just— Your girl friend stole forty thousand dollars.

Sam: What're you talking about? What is this?

Lila: She was supposed to bank it on Friday for her boss. And she didn't. And no one has seen her since.

Arbogast: Someone has seen her. Someone always sees a girl with forty thousand dollars!

Lila: Sam, they don't want to prosecute. They just want the money back.

Lila: Sam, if she's here—

Sam: She isn't! She isn't.

Arbogast: Miss Crane, can I ask you a question? Did you come up here on just a hunch and nothing more?

Lila: Not even a hunch. Just hope.

Arbogast: Well, with a little checking, I could get to believe you.

Lila: I don't care if you believe me or not! All I want to do is see Marion before she gets in this too deeply!

Sam: Did you check in Phoenix? Hospitals? Maybe she had an accident. Or a hold-up!

Arbogast: No—she was seen leaving town in her own car—by her employer, I might add.

Sam: I can't believe it. Can you?

Arbogast: Well, you know we're always quickest to doubt people who have a reputation for being honest. I think she's here, Miss Crane.

Arbogast: Where there's a boy friend—Well, she's not back there with the nuts and bolts but she's here in this town—somewhere. I'll find her. I'll be seeing you.

Arbogast: Good evening.
Norman: Evening.
Arbogast: I almost drove right past.

Norman: I'm always forgetting to turn the sign on, but we do have a vacancy. Twelve, in fact.
Arbogast: Oh—
Norman: Twelve cabins—twelve vacancies. Some candy?
Arbogast: No, thanks.

Arbogast: Uh—the last two days I've been to so many motels that my eyes are bleary with neon, but, y'know, this is the first place that looks like it's hiding from the world.

Norman: Well, I'll tell you the truth. I didn't really forget to turn the sign on. It just—it just doesn't seem like any use anymore, you know?
Arbogast: Oh?
Norman: You see, that used to be the main highway right there.

Norman: Well—d'you want to come in and register?
Arbogast: No, no-no. Sit down. I don't want to trouble you. I just want to ask you a few questions.

Norman: Oh, that's no trouble. Uh—today's linen day. I always change the beds here once a week whether they've been used or not. Hate the smell of dampness, don't you?
Arbogast: Mmm.

Norman: It's such a—I don't know—crazy smell. Come on.
Arbogast: Um-hm.

Norman: You uh—you out to buy a motel?
Arbogast: No.
Norman: Reason I asked, you said you'd seen so many in the past couple of days, I thought maybe you uh—What uh—what was it you wanted to ask?

Arbogast: Well—you see, I'm looking for a missing person. My name's Arbogast. I'm a private investigator.
Norman: Oh?

Arbogast: I've been trying to trace a girl that's been missing for—oh, about a week now—from Phoenix. It's a private matter—the family wants to forgive her. She's not in any trouble.
Norman: I didn't think the police went looking for people who aren't in trouble.

Arbogast: Oh, I'm—I'm not the police.
Norman: Oh, yeh.
Arbogast: We have reason to believe that she—came along this way and may have stopped in the area. Did she stop here?

Norman: Well, no one's stopped here for a couple of weeks.
Arbogast: Oh. Would you mind looking at the picture before committing yourself?

Norman: Commit myself? You sure talk like a policeman!
Arbogast: Well, look at the picture, please.

Norman: Uh-uh.
Arbogast: Sure?
Norman: Yeh.

Arbogast: Well, she may have used an alias. Uh—Marion Crane's her real name, but she could've registered under a different one.

Norman: Well, I'll tell you, I don't even—even much bother with uh—guests registering anymore. You know, one by one you drop the formalities. Uh—I shouldn't even bother changing the sheets, but—old habits die hard. Which reminds me.

Arbogast: What's that?
Norman: The lights—the sign.
Arbogast: Oh.

Norman: We had a couple last week said if the thing hadn't been on they would have thought this was an old deserted—

Arbogast: Well, you see—and that's exactly my point! And you said that nobody'd been here for a couple of weeks and there's a couple came by and—

Norman: Yeh.
Arbogast: —they didn't know that you were open.
Norman: Yeh.

Arbogast: Well, as you say, old habits die hard. It's possible this girl could have registered under another name. Do you mind if I look at your book?
Norman: No.

Arbogast: Thank you. Now let's see. Now here's the date somewhere—Um-hm.
Norman: See—there's nobody.

Arbogast: Yeh, I see. Now let's see what we have here. Now do I have a sample of her—handwriting here.

Arbogast: Oh, yes. Here we are. Marie Samuels. That's an interesting alias.

Norman: Is that her?
Arbogast: Yeh, I think so. Marie—Marion—Samuels. Her boy friend's name is Sam.

Norman: Hm.

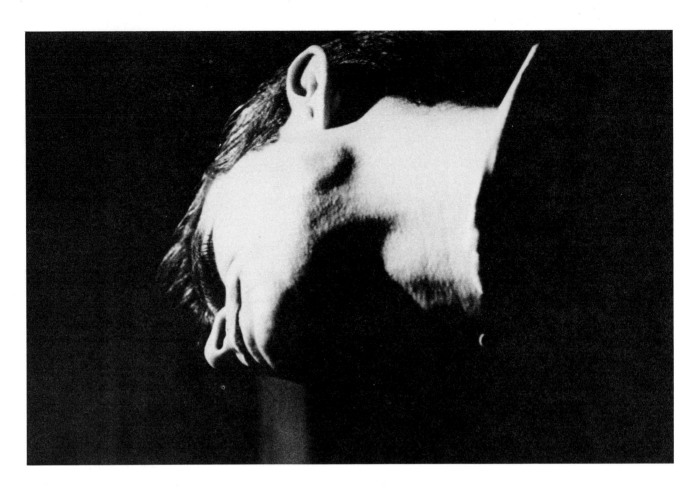

Arbogast: Um-hm. Was she in disguise by any chance?

Arbogast: Want to check the picture again?

Norman: Look, I-I-I wasn't lying to you, mister, it's just that—
Arbogast: Oh, I know that. I know you wouldn't lie.
Norman: You know, it's tough keepin' track of the time around here—
Arbogast: Oh, I know, I know.

Norman: Oh, yeah! Well, it-it wa- it was raining and uh— her hair was all wet.

Norman: I tell you, it's not—it's not really a very good picture of her either.

Arbogast: No, I guess not. Now tell me all about her.

Norman: Well, uh—she arrived uh—rather late one night, and she—went straight to sleep and uh—left early the next morning.

Arbogast: Well, how early?
Norman: Oh, very early.
Arbogast: Um-hm. Which morning was that?
Norman: Uh—the uh—th-th-th-th-th-th-th-the next morning—Sunday.

Arbogast: I see. Um-hm. Uh—did anyone meet her here?
Norman: No.
Arbogast: Did she arrive with anyone?
Norman: Mm-no.
Arbogast: Um-hm. She make any phone calls or—
Norman: No.

Arbogast: —locally?
Norman: Hm-um.
Arbogast: Did you spend the night with her?
Norman: No.
Arbogast: Well, then—how would you know that she didn't make any phone calls?

Norman: Oh, w-we-—well, she was very tired a-and uh—See, I—and I'm starting t-to uh—remember it. I-I'm making a mental picture of it in my mind. You know, you can make a mental picturization of something—in your sub-conscious.

Arbogast: That's right. And that takes time.
Norman: Uh—she was—she was sitting back there—

Norman: No-no, she was standing back there with a sandwich in her hand—and she said uh—she had to go to sleep early because she had uh—a long—d-d-d-dr-drive uh—ahead of her.

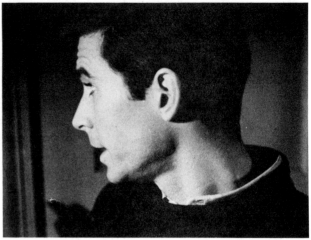

Arbogast: Um-hm. Back where?
Norman: Back there where she came from.
Arbogast: No. No, you said before that she was uh—sitting back there—
Norman: Oh, uh—
Arbogast: —or standing—

Norman: —yes. B-back in my uh—in my parlor there. Uh—she was very hungry and I made her a sandwich. And then she said uh—that she was tired and she uh—uh had to go uh—back to bed.

Arbogast: Oh, I see. Uh—how did she pay you? Cash? Check?

Norman: Cash.
Arbogast: Oh, cash, huh? Um-hm. And uh—after she left she uh—didn't come back?

Norman: Huh-uh. Well, why should she?

Arbogast: Yeah.

Norman: Well, Mr. Arbogast, uh—I guess that's about it, ain't it, eh? I've got some work to do, if you don't mind.

Arbogast: Well, to tell you the truth, I do mind. You see, if it doesn't jell, it isn't aspic. And this ain't jelling. It's not coming together. Something's missing.

Norman: Well, I—I don't know what you ex-—could expect me to know. People just come and go, you know.
Arbogast: That's right.

Arbogast: She isn't still here, is she?
Norman: No.
Arbogast: Um-hm.

Arbogast: If I wanted to uh—check the cabins—all twelve of them—I'd need a warrant, wouldn't I?
Norman: Listen, if you don't believe me, come on. Come on with me, and you can help me change beds—okay?

Arbogast: Oh—oh—well, thanks.

Norman: Oh-uh, change your mind?
Arbogast: Oh.

Norman: You know—I think I must have one of those faces you just can't help believing.
Arbogast: Is anyone at home?
Norman: No.

Arbogast: Oh, well, there's somebody sitting up in the window.
Norman: No, no, no, there isn't.
Arbogast: Oh, sure there is. Take a look.

Arbogast: Oh, I see. Well, now if this uh — girl, Marion Crane, were here, you wouldn't be hiding her, would you?
Norman: No.
Arbogast: Not even if she paid you well?
Norman: No.

Arbogast: Well, then —
Norman: And I'm not capable of being fooled! N-not even by a woman!
Arbogast: Well, it's not a slur on your manhood. I'm sorry.

Norman: Oh, th-that uh — that must be my mother. She's-she's in there — an invalid — an invalid. Uh — it's uh — practically like living alone.

Arbogast: Let's just say for the uh — just for the sake of argument — that she wanted you to gallantly protect her — you'd know that you were being used — that uh — you wouldn't be made a fool of, would you?
Norman: Well, I'm — I'm not a fool.

Norman: Now let's put it this way. She might have fooled me — but she didn't fool my mother.

Arbogast: Well, then your mother met her. Could I—could I talk to your mother?
Norman: No. As-as I told you, she's—she's confined.
Arbogast: Yes, but just for a few minutes, that's all. There might be some hint that you missed out on.

Arbogast: You know--sick old women are usually pretty sharp—
Norman: Now, mis—mister—
Arbogast: Just a moment. I wouldn't disturb her.
Norman: —Mister Arbogast, I—I think I've—I think I've talked to you all I want to.

Arbogast: Yes, but just for—
Norman: So I think it'd be much better if you left now.
Arbogast: Uh—All right. All right. You sure would save me a lot of leg-work if you'd let me talk to her about—Do I need a warrant for that, too?
Norman: Sure.

Arbogast: Uh-hm. All right. Thanks anyway.

Arbogast: Oh, hello. Loomis? This is Arbogast. Is uh— Lila there? Say, let me talk to her, please. Hello, Lila. Lila, listen. Marion was up there. Yes. She spent last Saturday night at the Bates Motel. It's right out here on the old highway. I even know what cabin she was in. It was Number One. Well, this young fellow that uh runs the place said that she just spent the night—left the next day and that was it. Mm. Uh—no, not exactly. Well, I did question him, believe me, but uh—I think I got all there was to get. I'll just have to pick up the pieces from here. Well, I tell you, I don't feel uh—entirely satisfied. Uh—See, this boy had a sick old mother. I think she saw Marion and talked to her. No. No, unfortunately, he wouldn't let me see her. Well, I was, but uh—I think I'll go back to the motel first. No—you stay there with Loomis. I'll be back in about an hour. All right, fine. Listen, I— You'll be happy to know what I think. Uh—I think our friend uh—Sam Loomis didn't know that Marion was here. Yeah. All right. See you in about an hour. Or less. Right. 'Bye-bye.

Arbogast: Bates?

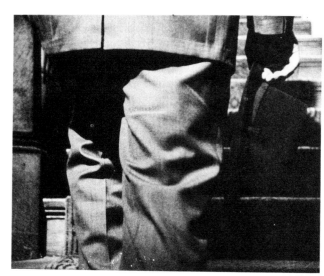

175

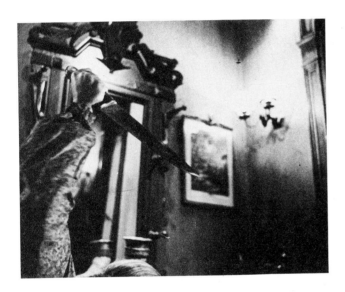

Sam: Sometimes Saturday night has a lonely sound. Ever notice that, Lila?

Lila: Sam, he said an hour—or less.
Sam: Yeh. It's been three.

Lila: Well, are we just going to sit here and wait?

Sam: He'll be back. Let's sit still and hang on, okay?

182

Lila: How far is the old highway?
Sam: You want to run out there, don't you? Bust in on Arbogast and the old lady, —
Lila: Yes, yes!

Sam: —and maybe shake her up? That wouldn't be a wise thing to do.

Lila: Patience doesn't run in my family, Sam. I'm going out there!
Sam: But Arbogast said—
Lila: An hour—or less!

Lila: Well, I'm going!

Sam: You'll never find it. Stay here.

Lila: Why can't I go with you?
Sam: I don't know,—One of us has to be here in case he's on the way.
Lila: Well, what am I supposed to do? Just sit here and wait?

Sam: Yeah.

Sam: Arbogast?! Arbogast!

Sam: Arbogast!!

Sam: He didn't come back here?
Lila: Sam!
Sam: No Arbogast—no Bates. Only the old lady at home.
A sick old lady unable to answer the door—or unwilling.

Lila: Where could he have gone?
Sam: Maybe he got some definite lead. Maybe he went right on.
Lila: Without calling me?
Sam: In a hurry.
Lila: Sam, he called when he had nothing! Nothing but a dissatisfied feeling! Don't you think he'd have called if he had anything at all?
Sam: Yes, I think he would have. Let's go see Al Chambers.
Lila: Who is he?
Sam: Our Deputy Sheriff around here.

Lila: All right. Let me get my coat.

Sam: Good evening. Well, I—I don't know where to start—except at the beginning.
Lila: Yes.

Sam: This is Lila Crane, from Phoenix.
Lila: How do you do?
Sam: She's been here searching for her sister. There's this private detective helping and—

Sam: Well, we got a call from this detective—saying that he'd traced her to that motel out on the old highway—

Mrs. Chambers: That must be the Bates Motel.

Sam: He traced her there and called us to say he was going to question Mrs. Bates.

Mrs. Chambers: Norman took a wife?

Sam: No, I don't think so. Uh-uh—an old woman. Uh—his mother. Well, anyway, that was early this evening. We haven't seen or heard from him since.
Sheriff: Now. Your sister's missin' how long?

Lila: Well, she left Phoenix a week ago yesterday—without a trace—

Sheriff: How'd you and this detective come to trace her to Fairvale?

Sam: They thought she'd be coming to me.
Sheriff: Left Phoenix under her own steam?
Lila: Yes.

Sheriff: She's not missin' so much as she's run away.
Sam: That's right.
Sheriff: From what?

Lila: She stole some money.

Sheriff: A lot?
Lila: Forty thousand dollars.
Sheriff: And the police haven't been able to—

Sam: Everyone concerned thought—that if they could get her to give the money back—they could avoid involving her with the police.

Sheriff: Well, that explains the private detective. He traced her to the Bates place. What exactly did he say when he called you?

Lila: Well, he said that Marion was there and uh—for one night, and then she left.
Sheriff: With the forty thousand dollars?

Lila: Well, he didn't say anything about the money. Well, it isn't important what he said on the phone, is it? He was supposed to come back here and talk to us after he talked to the mother, and he didn't! That's what I want you to do something about!

Sheriff: Like what?
Lila: Oh, I'm sorry if I seem overanxious! It's just that I'm sure there's something wrong out there and I have to know what!

Sheriff: Well, I think there's somethin' wrong, too, Miss. But not the same thing. I think what's wrong is your private detective. I think he got himself a hot lead as to where your sister was goin'—probably from Norman Bates and called you to keep you still while he took off after her and the money!

Lila: No! No, he said he was dissatisfied and he was going back there.

Mrs. Chambers: Why don't you call Norman and let him say just what happened?
Sheriff: At this hour?

Sam: Well, he was out when I was there just a while ago. Why, if he's back, he probably isn't even in bed yet.

Sheriff: He wasn't out when you were there. He just wasn't answerin' the door in the dead of night, like some people do.

Sheriff: This fellow lives like a hermit.

Sheriff: You must remember that bad business out there —about ten years ago?

Lila: Please! Call.

Mrs. Chambers: Florrie? The Sheriff wants you to connect him with the Bates Motel. Uh—

Sheriff: Oh, Norman? Sheriff Chambers. Ye—Oh, I been just fine, thanks. Listen, we got worries here. Yeh. Have you uh—had a feller stop by there tonight? Well, this one wouldn't be a customer, anyway. He's a private detective, name of—

Lila: Arbogast.
Sheriff: Arbogast. We—Yeh, and after he left? No, that's —that's okay, Norman.

Sheriff: This detective was there and Norman told him about the girl, the detective thanked him and he went away.

Lila: And he didn't come back? Didn't see the mother?

Sheriff: Your detective told you he couldn't come right back because he was goin' to question Norman Bates' mother. Right?

Lila: Yes.

Sheriff: Norman Bates' mother has been dead and buried in Greenlawn Cemetery for the past ten years!

Mrs. Chambers: I helped Norman pick out the dress she was buried in. Periwinkle blue.

Sheriff: 'Tain't only local history, Sam. It's the only case of murder and suicide on Fairvale ledgers.

Sheriff: Mrs. Bates poisoned this guy she was— involved with, when she found out he was married, —

Sheriff: then took a helpin' of the same stuff herself. Strychnine. Ugly way to die.

Mrs. Chambers: Norman found them dead together. In bed.

Sam: You mean that old woman I saw sittin' in the window out there wasn't Bates' mother?

Sheriff: Now, wait a minute, Sam. Are you sure you saw an old woman?

Sam: Yes! In the house behind the motel! I called and pounded but she just ignored me!

Sheriff: And you want to tell me you saw Norman Bates' mother?

Lila: But it had to be! Because Arbogast said so, too! And the young man wouldn't let him see her because she was too ill!

Sheriff: Well, if the woman up there is Mrs. Bates,— who's that woman buried out in Greenlawn Cemetery?

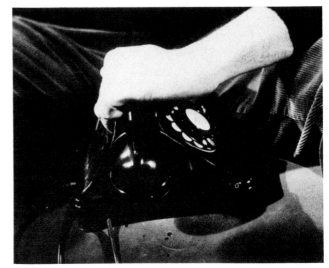

196

Norman: Well, mother. I . . . I'm gonna bring something up . . .

Mother: I am sorry boy, but you do manage to look ludicrous when you give me orders.
Norman: Please mother!

Mother: No, I will not hide in the fruit cellar. Ha! You think I'm fruity, ha! I'm staying right here. This is my room and no one will drag me out of it, least of all my big, bold son!

Norman: Now come now, mother! He came after the girl and someone will come after him! Mother, please! It's just for a few days. Just for a few days so they won't find you.

198

Mother: Just for a few days! In that dark, damp fruit cellar! No! You hid me there once and you won't do it again. Not ever again! Now get out! I told you to get out, boy!

Norman: I'll carry you, mother.
Mother: Norman, what do you think you're doing?

Mother: Don't you touch me! Don't! Norman! Put me down, put me down! I can walk with my own . . .

Sam: Good morning.
Sheriff & Mrs. Chambers: Good morning.
Sam: We thought if you didn't mind, we'd go out to that motel with you.
Mrs. Chambers: He's already been.

Sheriff: I went out before service.
Mrs. Chambers: Have you two had breakfast?
Sam: You didn't find anything?
Sheriff: Nothing. Let's clear the way here.

Lila: Well, what did he say about my sister?
Sheriff: Just what he told your detective. She used a fake name. Saw the register myself. Saw the whole place, as a matter of fact. That boy is alone there.

Sam: No mother?
Sheriff: You must've seen an illusion, Sam. Now, I know you're not the seein'-illusions type—but no woman was there and I don't believe in ghosts, so—

Lila: I—
Sheriff: —there it is.
Lila: —still feel that there's something—
Sheriff: Can see you do. I'm sorry I couldn't make you feel better.

Sheriff: You want to come around to my office this afternoon and report a missin' person and a theft, is what you want to do. The sooner you drop this in the lap of the law, that's the sooner you stand a chance of your sister bein' picked up. How about that?
Lila: I don't know.

Mrs. Chambers: It's Sunday. Come on over to the house and do your reporting around dinner time. It'll make it nicer.

Mrs. Chambers: You, too, Sam.
Sam: Thank you.

Sam: Maybe I am the seeing-illusions type.

Lila: No, you're not!

Sam: Well, do you want me to drop you at the hotel or—
Lila: Sam,—I still won't feel satisfied until I go out there!

Sam: Neither will I. Come on.

Sam: We better decide what we're gonna say or do when we walk in there.

Lila: We're going to register as man and wife. We're going to get shown to a cabin—and then we're gonna search every inch of the place—inside and out!

Sam: I wonder where Norman Bates does his hermiting.
Lila: Someone's at that window. I just saw the curtain move.

Sam: Come on.

Norman: Hello.
Sam: I was just coming up to ring for you.
Norman: Oh. I suppose you want a room.

Sam: We were gonna try to make it straight to San Francisco, but uh—we don't like the look of that sky. Looks like a bad day coming, doesn't it?
Norman: Okay.

Norman: I'll take you to Cabin Ten.
Sam: Better sign in first, hadn't we?
Norman: No, that's not necessary.

Sam: Huh–uh! My boss is paying for this trip, and uh— Well, it's ninety percent business and he wants practically notarized receipts. So uh—I'd better sign in and get a receipt.

Norman: Thank you. I'll get your bags.

Sam: Haven't any.

Norman: Well, I'll show you the room then.

Sam: First time I've ever seen it happen.

Sam: You check in any other place in this country without bags and you have to pay in advance.

Norman: Ten dollars.

Sam: That receipt?

Lila: I'll go on ahead.

Sam: Don't bother yourself. We'll find it.

Lila: Sam, we have to go into that cabin and search it, no matter what we're afraid of finding or how much it may hurt.
Sam: I know. Do you think if something happened, it happened there?

Lila: I don't know. But if you had a useless business like this motel, what would you need to get out? To get a new business somewhere else? Forty thousand dollars?

Sam: How could we prove that—Well, if he opens a motel on the new highway,—say a year—

Lila: There must be some proof that exists now! Something that proves he got that money away from Marion—somehow!

Sam: What makes you sound so certain?

Lila: Arbogast! He liked me, Sam! Or he felt sorry for me and he was beginning to feel the same way about you. I could tell the last time I talked to him on the phone. He wouldn't have gone anywhere or done anything without telling us, unless he was stopped! And he was stopped—so he must have found out something!

Sam: We'll start with Cabin One.

Sam: If he sees us, we're just taking the air.

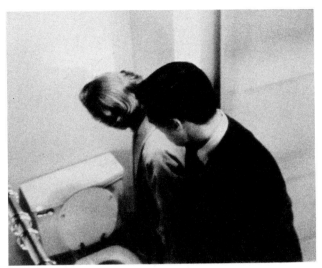

Sam: Bates?

Sam: There's no shower curtain.

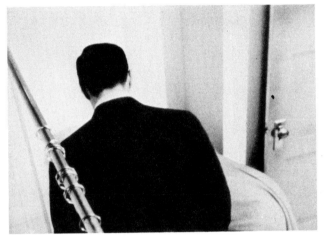

Lila: Sam!
Sam: What?
Lila: Look!
Sam: What is it?

Lila: Figuring! It didn't get washed down! Look. Some figure has been added to or subtracted from forty thousand! That proves Marion was here! It'd be too wild a coincidence—

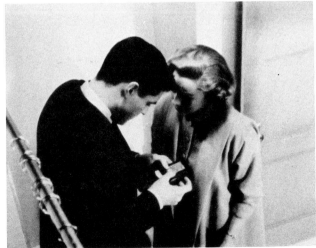

Sam: Bates never denied she was here.
Lila: Oh. Doesn't that prove that he found out about the money?
Sam: Do we simply ask him where he's hidden it?

Lila: No. But that old woman—whoever she is—she told Arbogast something. I want her to tell us the same thing!

213

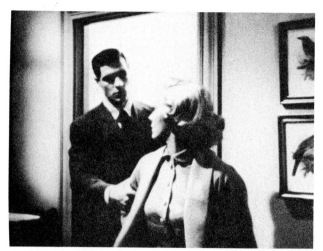

Sam: You can't go up there!
Lila: Why not?

Sam: Bates.
Lila: Well, let's find him. One of us can keep him occupied while the other gets to the old woman.

Sam: You'll never be able to hold him still if he doesn't want to be held! And I don't like you going into that house alone, Lila.
Lila: I can handle a sick old woman!
Sam: All right. I'll find Bates and keep him occupied.

Sam: Wait a minute! If you get anything out of the mother,—Can you find your way back to town?
Lila: Yes, of course.
Sam: Well, if you do get anything,—don't stop to tell me.

Norman: You looking for me?

Sam: Why, yes, as a matter of fact. The—wife's taking a nap and—I never can keep quiet enough for her so I— just thought I'd look you up and talk.

Norman: Good. You're satisfied with your cabin?
Sam: Oh, it's fine!

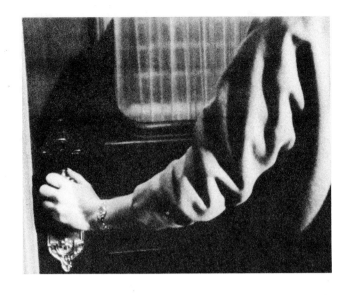

Sam: I'm not saying you shouldn't be contented here, I'm just doubting that you are. I think if you saw a chance to get out from under you would unload this place.

Norman: This place! This place happens to be my only world. I grew up in that house up there. I happen to have had a very happy childhood. My mother and I were more than happy.

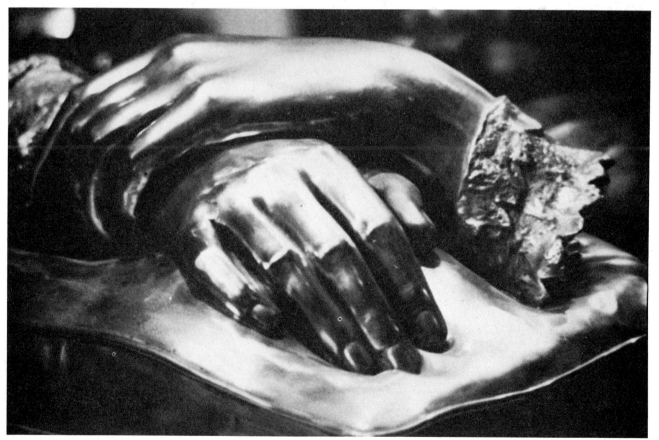

Sam: You look frightened, have I been saying something frightening?
Norman: I don't know what you've been saying.

Sam: I've been talking about your mother, about your motel. Are you going to do it?
Norman: Do what?

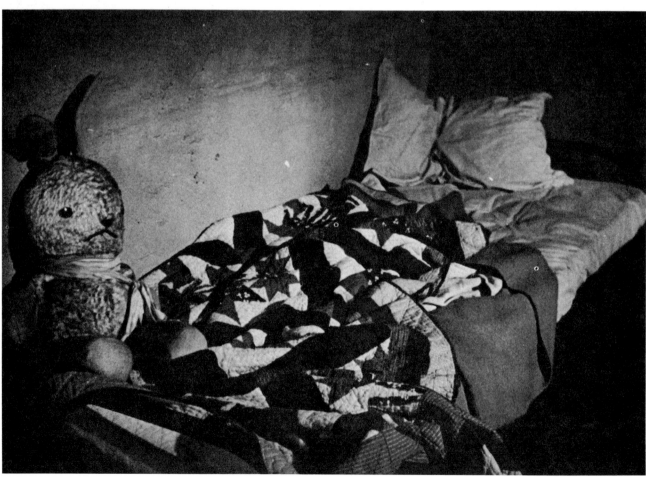

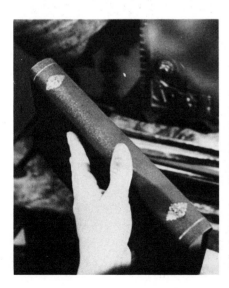

Sam: In a new town you won't have to hide your mother.

Norman: Why don't you get in your own car and drive away from here?

Norman: Okay?
Sam: Where will you get the money to do that, Bates, or do you already have it socked away?

Norman: Shut up.

Sam: A lot of money—$40,000. I bet your mother knows where the money is and what you did to get it. I think she will tell us.

Norman: Where's that girl you came here with? Where is she?

 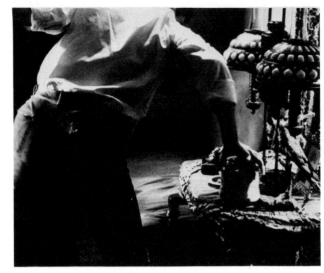

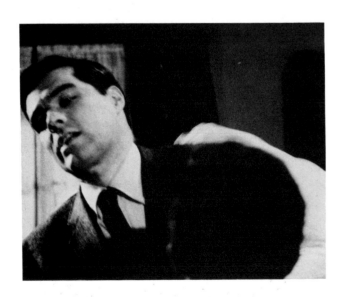 

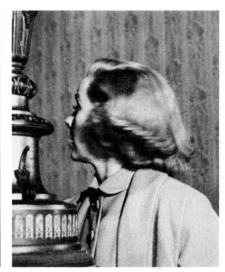

Lila: Mrs. Bates?

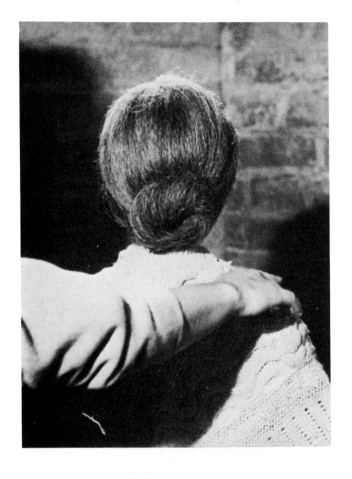 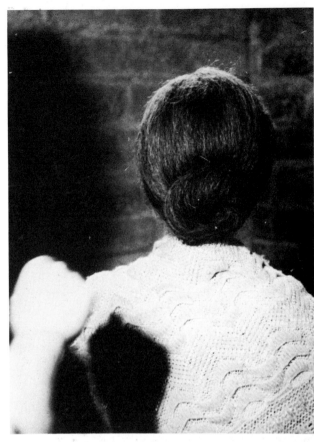

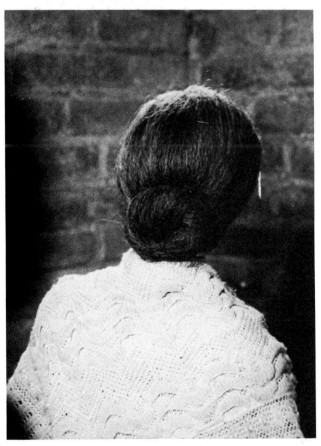 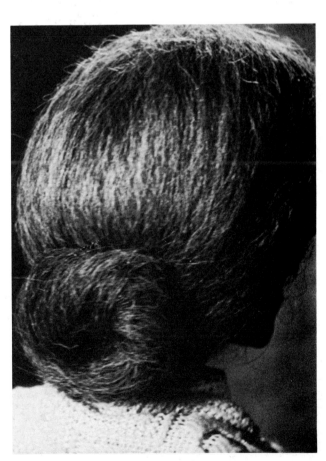

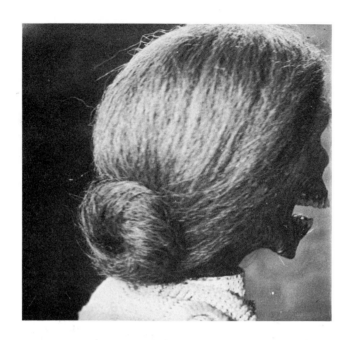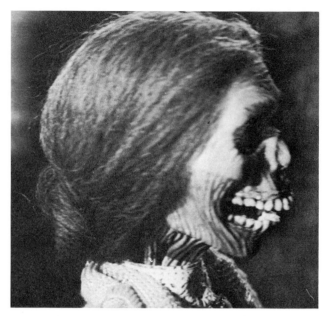

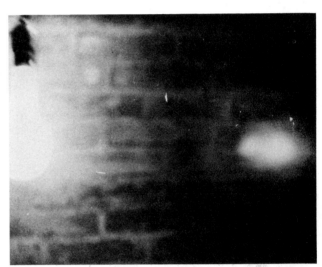

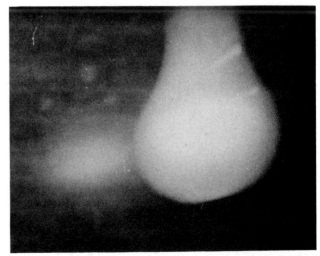

Sheriff: Well, if anyone gets any answers it'll be the psychiatrist. Even I couldn't get to Norman, and he knows me. You warm enough, Miss?
Lila: Yes.

District Attorney: Did he talk to you?
Dr. Richman: No. I got the whole story—but not from Norman.

Dr. Richman: I got it—from his mother.

Dr. Richman: Norman Bates no longer exists.

Dr. Richman: He only half-existed to begin with.

Dr. Richman: And now, the other half has taken over. Probably for all time.

Lila: Did he kill my sister?

Richman: Yes,—and no.

District Attorney: Well, now look, if you're trying to lay some psychiatric groundwork for some sort of plea this fellow would like to cop—

Richman: A psychiatrist doesn't lay the groundwork. He merely tries to explain it.

Lila: But my sister is —

Richman: Yes. Yes, I'm sorry. The private investigator, too.

Richman: If you drag that swamp somewhere in the vicinity of the motel, you'll — Uh — have you any unsolved missing persons cases on your books?

Chief of Police: Yes. Two.
Richman: Young girls?
Chief of Police: Did he confess to —

Richman: Like I said, — the mother —

Richman: Now to understand it the way I understood it, hearing it from the mother, — that is, from the mother half of Norman's mind — you have to go back ten years, — to the time when Norman murdered his mother and her lover.

Richman: Now he was already dangerously disturbed, — had been ever since his father died. His mother was a clinging, demanding woman, and for years the two of them lived as if there was no one else in the world.

Richman: Then she met a man—and it seemed to Norman that she 'threw him over' for this man. Now that pushed him over the line and he killed 'em both.

Richman: Matricide is probably the most unbearable crime of all—most unbearable to the son who commits it. So he had to erase the crime, at least in his own mind. He stole her corpse. A weighted coffin was buried.

Richman: He hid the body in the fruit cellar. Even treated it to keep it as well as it would keep. And that still wasn't enough. She was there! But she was a corpse. So he began to think and speak for her, give her half his life, so to speak.

Richman: At times he could be both personalities, carry on conversations. At other times, the mother half took over completely. Now he was never all Norman, but he was often only mother.

Richman: And because he was so pathologically jealous of her, he assumed that she was as jealous of him. Therefore, if he felt a strong attraction to any other woman, the mother side of him would go wild.

Richman: When he met your sister, he was touched by her —aroused by her.

Richman: He wanted her.

Richman; That set off the 'jealous mother' and 'mother killed the girl!'

Richman: Now after the murder, Norman returned as if from a deep sleep.

Richman: And like a dutiful son, covered up all traces of the crime he was convinced his mother had committed!

Sam: Well, why was he—dressed like that?

District Attorney: He's a transvestite!

Richman: Ah, not exactly.

Richman: A man who dresses in women's clothing in order to achieve a sexual change, or satisfaction, is a transvestite.

Richman: But in Norman's case, he was simply doing everything possible to keep alive the illusion of his mother being alive.

Richman: And when reality came too close,—when danger or desire threatened that illusion—he dressed up, even to a cheap wig he bought.

Richman: He'd walk about the house, sit in her chair, speak in her voice. He tried to be his mother!

Richman: And uh—now he is.

Richman: Now that's what I meant when I said I got the story from the mother. You see, when the mind houses two personalities,

Richman: there's always a conflict, a battle.

Richman: In Norman's case, the battle is over,—and the dominant personality has won.

Sheriff: And the forty thousand dollars? Who got that?

Richman: The swamp. These were crimes of passion, not profit.

Police Guard: He feels a little chill. Can I bring him this blanket?

Richman: Oh, sure.
Chief of Police: All right.

Mother's Voice: Thank you.

253

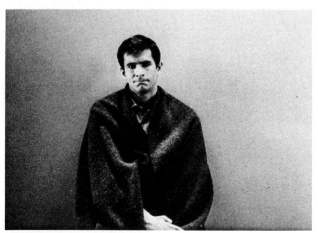

Mother's Voice: *It is sad when a mother has to speak the words that condemn her own son.*

Mother's Voice: *I can't allow them to think I would commit murder. Put him away now as I should have years ago. He was always bad and in the end he intended to tell them I killed those girls and that man,*

Mother's Voice: *as if I could do anything but just sit and stare like one of his stuffed birds. They know I can't move a finger and I want to just sit here and be quiet just in case they suspect me. They are probably watching me—well, let them.*

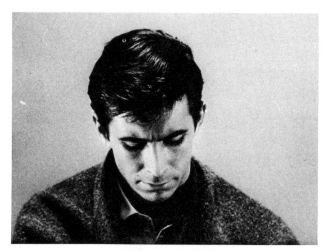

Mother's Voice: *Let them see what kind of person I am—*

254

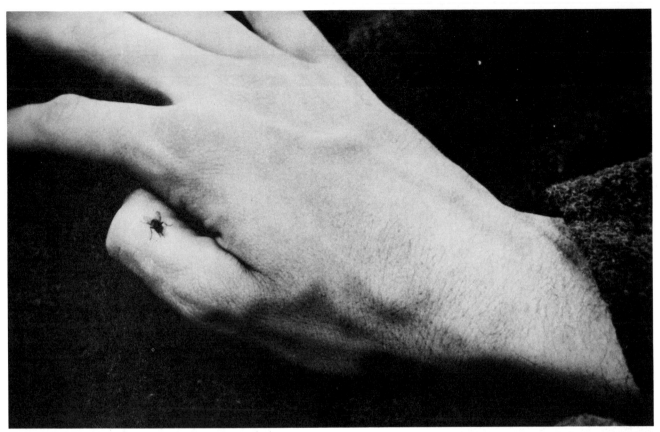

Mother's Voice: *not even going to swat that fly.*

Mother's Voice: *I hope that they are watching, they will see, they will see and they will say "why she wouldn't even harm*

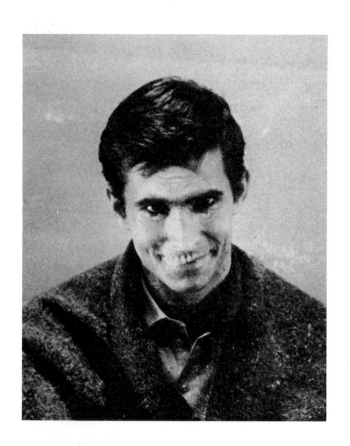

THE END